BUTCH CASSIDY
∾ and other ∾
MORMON
OUTLAWS
OF THE OLD WEST

OTHER BOOKS AND AUDIO BOOKS
BY KATHRYN JENKINS GORDON

The Essential Book of Mormon Companion
A Father's Greatest Gift
The First Nativity
My Redeemer Lives

BUTCH CASSIDY
∽ and other ∽
MORMON
OUTLAWS
OF THE OLD WEST

Kathryn Jenkins Gordon

Covenant Communications, Inc.

Published by Covenant Communications, Inc.
American Fork, Utah

Printed in the United States of America
First Printing: May 2013

19 18 17 16 15 14 13   10 9 8 7 6 5 4 3

ISBN 978-1-62108-119-7

DEDICATION

To Glenn,
who shows such interest in everything I do;
to Jessica, Nicholas, and Melissa,
who believe I can do anything;
to Ryan, who shows me daily
what determination and faith can do;
and to Brooklyn, Noah, and Charlotte—
may you never lose your sense of wonder,
and may your imagination
continue to grow as you do.

ACKNOWLEDGMENTS

THERE ARE SO MANY TO thank on a project like this. First and foremost, my thanks to Barry Evans, whose interest in Mormon outlaws was the genesis for this book. Listening to his enthusiasm and imagination fired my own.

Many thanks to the scholars and researchers whose dogged determination resulted in much of the information we know about these outlaws. Their work informed my efforts, and I am grateful for their diligent labors. Their names appear in the Endnotes.

Much gratitude goes to John A. Bascom of Apple Valley, California—a direct descendant of many who lived the stories you'll read about on these pages—for his generous help on this project. He provided rich detail, told delightful stories, and pillaged his personal collection to share the family photos of the lawmen who cavorted with and sometimes arrested the outlaws.

Last, but certainly not least, a nod to the Mormons of the Old West—those who made their way across the godforsaken plains to their new Zion, those who stepped up to enforce the law in the vast recesses of the frontier, and those who made it necessary to enforce the law: the outlaws. Your stories have piqued our imagination, inspired our collective histories, and left us staggered. May they never be forgotten.

TABLE OF CONTENTS

INTRODUCTION

MORMON OUTLAWS? THE VERY PHRASE seems like an oxymoron.

Sure. You know all about Mormons; you might even be one. Mormons—more accurately known as Latter-day Saints—are the people who live by the Golden Rule, elevating honesty and kindness to an absolute art form. According to their own Articles of Faith, they believe in being upstanding citizens wherever they live—in honoring, obeying, and sustaining the law. They watch out for one another. Take care of one another. Pairs of men and pairs of women watch over local congregations, making sure any needs are immediately taken care of.

At various points in their history, they lived a common law; everyone donated their crops and livestock to a communal storehouse, and the available goods were distributed on an as-needed basis. As they did then, they still work hard to abolish envy, jealously, anger, strife, and hatred from their ranks. Those emotions are replaced by love, compassion, forgiveness, and friendship. Known for their industry and fierce self-sufficiency, they also hang their hats on the Ten Commandments. No self-respecting, devout Mormon would ever consider stealing from another. Quite the opposite, they contribute generously in tithes and offerings to help others who might need assistance.

Once an obscure religion, The Church of Jesus Christ of Latter-day Saints has risen to national—and international—prominence. That's partly because of the missionary force, tens of thousands strong, who pound the pavement in the far reaches of the globe to spread their message of truth and salvation. And it's partly because of prominent Mormons in assorted areas of politics and business—among them people like hotel magnate J. Willard Marriott, Academy Award-winning producer Jerry

Molen, US Senate Majority Leader Harry Reid, baseball great Vance Law, businessman and philanthropist Larry H. Miller, Black & Decker CEO Nolan Archibald, and human relations guru Stephen R. Covey.

Let's face it: Wherever the Mormons are, they're known for honesty, integrity, morality, love of country, love of God, and love of fellow man. Hardly the things one normally associates with outlaws.

So it comes as a sort of shock to some that among the rough-riding, horse-stealing, cattle-rustling, bank-robbing, gun-slinging outlaws of the Old West were a fair number of Mormons. That's right. Mormons.

How on earth did THAT happen? you might be asking yourself. After all, the outlaws were such a . . . *different* sort of bunch. There was *nothing* law-abiding among those folks. Bottom on their list of priorities was sharing, taking care of others, lifting the arms that hang down. If they saw something they wanted, they took it—even if they had to pull a few triggers to accomplish the deed. One woman described the outlaws who surrounded her as people for whom total honesty was "a personal encumbrance."

Scarcely sounds like the typical Mormons. In fact, it bears no resemblance whatsoever.

But some of the outlaws *were* Mormons . . . and some of the Mormons *were* outlaws.

Like who? You'll read about some of them in this book. Some are household names. For example, nearly everyone has heard of, and knows something about, Orrin Porter Rockwell, Joseph Smith's boyhood friend and later bodyguard. As you'll read, he's a fascinating character. Sometimes he was the law, and other times he was the outlaw.

One of Utah's most famous native sons was Robert LeRoy Parker, born in 1866 in Beaver, Utah, the oldest of thirteen children of devout Mormon handcart pioneers. Attracted to a life of crime in his adolescence by friends who were cattle rustlers, he became known as Butch Cassidy—a colorful outlaw who eventually headed up the Wild Bunch, a gang of criminals who pulled off some of the most daring robberies in the nation's history. Oh, wait—fully one-third of his gang, twenty of the sixty or so bandits, were Mormons.

Another of Utah's best-known native sons was Willard Erastus Christianson, born in 1864 in Ephraim, Utah, the son of a Swedish father and a German mother who had come to Utah as Mormon converts. He devoutly practiced his faith while young, but while walking home from a Church dance one Saturday night he whacked a rival on the head with a rock. Erroneously fearing he had killed the lad, he believed his salvation was doomed—so he ran away from home, joined a band of cattle rustlers, and lived much of the rest of his life as an outlaw. Known as Matt Warner, "the Mormon Kid," he was only fourteen at the time. (Side note: You're never beyond redemption.)

Then there was John Thomas ("Tom") McCarty, also raised in a staunch Mormon family in Ephraim; he married Matt Warner's sister, Christina ("Tennie"), and actually mentored Matt in his life of crime. On March 30, 1889, Tom joined his two buddies—Matt Warner and Butch Cassidy—in pulling off one of the largest bank robberies of the day: They absconded with $20,000 from the First National Bank of Denver—just shy of $400,000 in today's currency.

Tom's behavior that day is typical for many of the Mormon outlaws—courtesy and gentility uncommon among most criminals. No brutal pistol-whipping or vulgarity here. On the day in question, Tom walked casually up to the bank president and quietly stated, "Excuse me, sir, but I just overheard a plot to rob this bank."

Alarmed, the bank president nervously replied, "Oh, no! How did you learn of this plot?"

With a smile spreading slowly across his face, Tom replied, "I planned it." Then, raising his gun, he politely stated the obvious: "Put up your hands." (Side note: Profanity is a sign of a weak vocabulary.)

There are more. Lots more.

Theirs was an upbringing that often peeked through the rough exteriors of the Mormon outlaws. They rustled cattle from a rancher's herd then paid the rancher generously to help drive the bounty to a secure hiding place. They shot up local saloons in drunken gunfights then returned the next day to pay a dollar a hole for damages. There was even a Robin Hood mentality that often manifested itself. Butch Cassidy, hearing of a farm that was threatened with foreclosure, went to the local bank and generously paid the poor farmer's mortgage. The next day he returned, robbing the bank to get back his money.

Few things capture our imaginations like these kinds of stories from the Old West—the exploits of horse thieves and bank robbers and the holdup men who ran roughshod in the first half-century after

Utah and the surrounding areas were settled. Throw religion into the mix, and you have the stuff of enduring legend . . . stories that defy the imagination and leave you shaking your head in wonder.

So sit back, relax, and read the tales that follow. You'll find out how the culture and attitudes of pioneer Utah actually contributed to a generation of Mormon outlaws—and why the Mormons didn't simply run the outlaws out of town. You'll find out who's who and what they did and where they hid. You'll even get a peek at the Mormon lawmen who dedicated their lives to pursuing the Mormon outlaws. And through it all, you're practically guaranteed to have a rip-roarin' good time!

CHAPTER ONE
Mormon Outlaws? How Did THAT Happen?

IN ANY DISCUSSION OF MORMONS and outlaws—at least in the early days of settlement—it's important to start at the very beginning.

It's really very simple: there were Mormon outlaws. And there were outlaw Mormons. Lots of them, really. Some of whom became very famous. Household names, so to say, even a century and a half later.

When you take into consideration the strict, conservative views and behavior of the sturdy folks who swelled the ranks of The Church of Jesus Christ of Latter-day Saints and made their way in the toughest manner possible across an unforgiving prairie, how on earth do you account for the fact that some of those intrepid pioneers and their children became outlaws? Even more puzzling, how is it possible that the Saints not only tolerated, but sometimes embraced, the sinners among them?

The answer takes us on a fascinating ride into the Territory of Utah during the second half of the nineteenth century—a place one sociologist called "a hotbed of two distinct cultural phenomena."[1] One, of course, was the very religious—sometimes pious—group of Mormon pioneers, the first of whom arrived in tattered companies in July 1847. The second seems at first glance to be the polar opposite, a group consisting of good old American outlaws: bank robbers, cattle rustlers, gunfighters, holdup men, murderers, and thieves. But a closer look reveals a wonder that seems to defy the senses—a hefty number of those outlaws were first Mormons, and bounded into notoriety out of the tightly knit group of Saints scattered among the Utah settlements.

Esteemed historian Wallace Stegner, well-known for his astute descriptions of early Mormon life in Utah, suggested that Mormon

Early map of the Territory of Utah, with the territory as it would have been during the active outlaw period.

outlaws were a sign of "a fairly frequent dissatisfaction among the young blades with the stodgy laboriousness of their homes."[2] Simply stated, adolescent boys were fed up with the rules and regulations of home. As any parent of a rebellious teen can attest, such an observation could certainly be founded on fact—a youth tired of the uptight restrictions of home may yearn for something different. But according to many who have studied the situation, there was much more to it than that. In fact, the link between Mormons and outlaws actually seems due to their similarities, not their differences.

One similarity between the two groups, of course, was location: while some Mormon outlaws eventually drifted to Idaho and California, most were concentrated in Utah. As we'll see in the next chapter, some of the rugged, isolated stretches of terrain in the Utah Territory almost begged to become protective outposts for the nation's most dogged lawbreakers. For a number of decades, after all, there was a stretch of a thousand miles or more between the Territory of Utah and the nearest outposts of civilization, complete with their determined law enforcement personnel and trusty sheriffs.

Within days of arriving in the Salt Lake Valley, Mormon pioneers drove stakes into the parched desert soil, figured out how to divert irrigation water from the nearby streams and rivers, and began to plow and sow crops from the seeds they had carried with them from the verdant Midwest. They plotted out towns and dedicated a site for a temple to their God. Lest the entire process sound too simple, know this: the desolate landscape of their promised land presented a ferocious struggle for the pioneers who resolved to there establish Zion.

That same desolate landscape—such a torment to the early settlers—became instead a blessing to the outlaws. No need to build elaborate garrisons or get creative about hiding places; the chiseled cliffs, craggy canyons, and rocky outposts created natural fortresses and hideouts for those on the wrong side of the law. The tiny communities scattered along the backbone of the Rocky Mountains at the colonizing direction of Brigham Young were so isolated that they became perfect sanctuaries for bank robbers and cattle rustlers. Harbored in the secluded little towns, outlaws simply dropped off the radar. Lawmen simply weren't interested enough, or equipped enough, to pursue lawbreakers into such insulated—and sometimes nearly inaccessible—hideaways. A perfect example was Robbers' Roost, a hiding place for outlaws that could be accessed only through a single narrow canyon that could be very efficiently guarded by a lone gunman.

Along with isolated geography came a distinct lack of population, which also fostered the outlaws. In 1880, more than thirty years after the Mormon pioneers arrived in the Salt Lake Valley, Utah's population averaged fewer than two people per square mile,[3] most of whom were concentrated in cities and townships throughout the Territory. The result was vast areas of land devoid of settlers—and law enforcement officers to boot. Every little town bank or area mine or passing train, then, was vulnerable to outlaws, a situation that didn't improve much until railroads and telegraph lines helped secure lonely outposts.

The Saints worked tirelessly to convert the stubborn territory into their own brand of Eden. It had been Brigham Young's intent to lead his people to a place where they would no longer be "polluted" by the rest of American society. He wanted a spot isolated and protected from the hordes who had persecuted and driven the Mormons from their earlier settlements—who had tarred and feathered, and eventually murdered, their Prophet. He wanted a place where his beleaguered people could withdraw and exist in solitary peace. Even more compelling than their common faith was their common bond forged by nearly unrelenting persecution over more than a decade.

Evidence indicates that Brigham considered several areas as possible settlements. One was California, but the discovery of gold had

Independence Rock—a huge granite outcropping measuring 130 feet high, 1,900 feet long, and 850 feet across—was one of the most notable landmarks on the emigrant trail to Utah. It is inscribed with the names of thousands of travelers who passed it on their journey.

swarms of "forty-niners" beating a path to the coastal region. It would never do. Another was Mexico, an area later colonized but rejected as a central destination. By divine directive, Brigham looked out from his vantage point in the hills above the Great Salt Lake and declared the desolate valley below to be the "right place." Somewhere in the back of his mind had to be the realization—and reassurance—that his band of Saints would be safe there, adequately removed from the people who had done them such harm. But furthest from his mind had to be the notion that he was establishing a hideout for outlaws, some of whom would spring up from among his own people.

The desire for isolation was clear, and at first the Saints were able to remain sequestered. But within a few years Salt Lake City found itself at the crossroads: it became a handy stopover for immigrants along the Oregon Trail looking for land to homestead as well as those headed to California in search of gold. It was the perfect place for people to stop, rest, and secure needed provisions to continue their journey. While that eventually proved to be an economic blessing to the Saints in Salt Lake, it also defeated Brigham Young's objective to keep them untainted from the sordid influences of American society at large. It also proved to be an unwitting draw for outlaws drifting through along with the rest of the immigrants; they recognized a fertile spot in which to put down roots, and put down roots they did.

So among the outlaw population, which came first—the outsiders who infiltrated the settlements, or the Mormons who rose up among them? It's hard to say, but one thing's clear: They encouraged each other until their numbers were large enough to be a force to be reckoned with among the Utah population.

But location was scarcely the only similarity between the Mormons and the outlaws. Cultural parallels between the two groups made it inevitable that they would eventually share members.

One factor was the early form of government in the Territory of Utah: the Saints were governed by a theocracy in which the Church governed all economic, political, agricultural, industrial, social, and spiritual aspects of life. Under that theocracy, the Church implemented a form of the United Order in which all agricultural products were stored in communal warehouses (bishops' storehouses) and distributed on an as-needed basis to the Mormons who labored for them. (Incidentally, this system initially made it very difficult for the Mormons to barter with immigrants passing through and needing provisions; they could not provide necessities to the immigrants without diminishing their own stores.[4])

But that wasn't the only thing that contributed to a sort of "community property" attitude in the territory. John A. Bascom—now a resident of Apple Valley, California, and the descendant of a whole passel of the earliest Mormon lawmen—explains that there was a "finder's keepers" attitude common to frontier living. It was, simply, a way of life, and there was nothing "wrong" or illegal about it.

The "finder's keepers" attitude of the frontier—typified by freely shooting any buffalo that were needed—was a way of life and is one of the factors that contributed to the "community property" attitude in the early Utah Territory.

When the settlers crossed the plains, Bascom points out, the buffalo were simply there for the taking. Land was settled at will—first come, first served. Deer and elk were hunted without limit; Bascom's father remembered men coming home from the hunt pulling wagons heaped with deer.

Wild, maverick cattle—"free-range cattle" that were not branded— were free for the taking to anyone who could catch them. Cowboys throughout the territory, Mormons and non-Mormons alike, carried running irons and rings for just such opportunities. Herds of wild horses, often called "Indian ponies," were also free for the taking. Bascom's ancestors, all well-respected lawmen, chased and gathered so many wild horses throughout Utah, Colorado, and Wyoming that the sale of the steeds paid for the family's move to Canada.

It wasn't just the animals that were considered fair game. Timber was there for the taking, cut down at will to use as building material. Gold, silver, gilsonite, and coal were freely available to any who wanted them. Oil and tar seeps were freely used.

In an atmosphere where so many were living so freely off the land for so long, it was easy for the eventual boundaries to be blurred.

And when those boundaries eventually were established and the federal government arrived in droves to enforce things, there was a

Early in the Utah Territory, "free-range cattle"—wild cattle that were not branded—roamed the area and were free to anyone who could catch them; for some, it was easy to make the leap from catching maverick cattle to rustling those that legitimately belonged to ranchers.

real "us versus them" mentality when it came to the government. "Us," ruled by a peaceful and God-sanctioned theocracy, were good; "them," the "others" who so often failed to protect "us," were bad. The band of people clustered in the Utah Territory—Mormons and outlaws alike—saw themselves as *right* and the federal government (and its law enforcement personnel) as *wrong*.

That's not all. A totally unintended result of the communal system among the Mormons was a decided disregard among some of them for the property of non-Mormons—an attitude that definitely was not encouraged or sanctioned by the Church but that seeped into some of the outlying regions. Captain J. W. Gunnison, who reported extensively and fairly objectively on the early settlements in Utah, wrote that some Mormons figured they could simply take possession of "Gentile" (non-Momron) property, and that "it would be no theft to secure cattle and grain from the neighboring pastures and fields" because "the inheritance of the earth belongs to the Saints."[5] They also figured they had it "coming to them" because of the injustices to which they were subjected by non-Mormons in Illinois and Missouri, even though their Gentile neighbors had nothing to do with those injustices.

The central Utah city of Gunnison, named after Captain J. W. Gunnison, was settled by cattle rustlers.

Simply taking what they wanted from non-Mormons was clearly a case of misinterpreted and misapplied doctrine that was prompted by insecurity and not just a little fear. When such practices were brought to the attention of Church leaders, the Saints were soundly corrected. Nonetheless, the practice—and attitude—persisted for many years, creating an atmosphere that helped foster the outlaws, Mormons among them.

Not too long after they settled their Zion, the Mormons in Utah came under the scrutiny of a passel of "reporters," writers eager to "investigate" new outposts of civilization and pass their observations on to the rest of the country. While several writers—Wallace Stegner among them—made a solid effort to understand the Mormons and commented favorably on the Saints and their settlement, few were known for their objectivity, and most didn't even try to disguise what could only be called animosity toward the Latter-day Saints. Most observers commented on cultural quirks that, in hindsight, undoubtedly at least contributed to an outlaw mentality among some. One observer sarcastically wrote that as long as "an occasional killing" against outsiders was not considered a crime, "then the Mormons are an exceptionally moral, virtuous, civil, cheerful, industrious and prosperous people." Then, referring to the way the courts favored the Mormons, he facetiously penned, "By the court records they are most exceptionally virtuous."[6]

Still another reporter, known for his distaste toward the Mormons, wrote that there was in Utah "more downright lying to the square mile than in any other region on this continent; and the religious lying is the worst of all."[7]

Even the children were not immune. Wait—how could the children of pioneers who crossed the plains with faith in every footstep grow up to become outlaws? Again, there's the matter of culture in the Territory of Utah. It's no surprise that the children who grew up in that environment developed a healthy dislike of and belligerence toward non-Mormons and an entitlement attitude toward their property. In our day, encouraged by the songs we sing in Primary, we think of those little boys and girls as the epitome of sweetness and innocence, conceived in faith and raised in righteousness. In truth, largely as a result of the prevailing culture, there was at least some outlaw-like behavior going on, even among the youth. Gunnison, known for his objectivity (and one of the only reporters friendly to the Mormons), wrote of those in the outlying areas, "Of all the children that have come under our observation, we must in candor say those of the Mormons are the most lawless and profane."[8] John D. Lee, who was eventually executed for his role in the Mountain Meadows Massacre, wrote about one of his rebellious sons that the children of his day "were begotten in the days of trial" and that "the spirit of alienation and disaffection were entailed upon the children."[9]

We know from reading the histories of our own ancestors countless stories of faith, determination, charity, and unflinching goodness. But as with any sizable group, there were those who reacted to the same adversities that made some into Saints by becoming clearly less than Saints—at least in some aspects of their lives. And those with even a slight propensity to rebellion against their religious parents or neighbors soon had plenty of opportunity to affiliate with a decidedly "outlaw" element. Not long after the Mormons set up house in the valley, a Major Jacob Holemann wrote to his superiors from his outpost in the eastern territory's Great Basin that he was in "great confusion" and wanted federal troops to help maintain order. The problem? Apparently significant numbers of outlaws had infiltrated the area—and "The *white* Indians, I apprehend, are much more dangerous than the red. The renegades, deserters, and thieves, who have had to fly from justice [on their way to] California, have taken refuge in the mountains, and having associated themselves with the Indians are more savage than the Indians themselves."[10]

Obviously, there was enough of a "bad element" among non-Mormons that any Saint who wanted to stray had ample opportunity to affiliate with an outlaw crowd. Over a several-decade period, the outlaws—Mormons among them—caused general havoc, especially in the outlying communities. The central Utah town of Gunnison, named after Captain J. W. Gunnison, was actually settled in the 1850s by a group of cattle rustlers.[11] And by 1885, according to the stories

By 1885, about half the residents of Circle Valley—a settlement on Fremont Island, shown here—were cattle rustlers.

of old-timers, about half the residents of Circle Valley, a settlement established on Fremont Island in the Great Salt Lake, were involved in the cattle-rustling industry.[12]

In many areas, in fact, there was little distinction between the lawless and the law-abiding. And it should be pointed out that the federal government itself contributed to blurring the distinction: Those Mormons who lived the law of plural marriage were branded as "outlaws" by federal officers who ruthlessly hunted down and arrested as many polygamist husbands and fathers as they could get their hands on.

In an attempt to live their religion in peace, a number of polygamists moved to more isolated areas where they hoped they would be free from prosecution. A perfect example is the still-picturesque Star Valley, Wyoming, just south of Jackson Hole and on the fringes of the present-

A group of Sugar House polygamist prisoners illustrates the situation that existed during the early days of the Utah Territory: the federal government, in its fervor to prosecute those who lived the law of plural marriage, blurred the lines between the lawless and the law-abiding.

day Utah border. Well off all the existing routes, it was originally settled by faithful and law-abiding polygamists who found in its mountainous isolation an ideal place to escape the scrutiny of federal officers. But they weren't the only ones who found perfect safety there—before long the cattle rustlers and bank robbers moved in and also felt perfectly safe from detection or arrest.[13]

The result? Not just in Star Valley but in dozens of isolated communities throughout Utah, the relationship between polygamist Mormons (considered "outlaws") and the *actual* outlaws (bank robbers, cattle rustlers, and worse) became very close.

Especially in the outlying regions, where most outlaw activity took place, there were so few people per square mile that the isolation was often intense. Cowboy Guy McNurlen was summoned to court one day to testify against Ann Bassett of Brown's Hole, accused of rustling cattle and changing the brands on their hides. As he signed in to provide his testimony, McNurlen listed his address only as "the chuckwagon."

Some of the benches and tablelands were so isolated, Bascom remembers, that visitors had a tough time accessing them. They couldn't even reach them on horseback. The steep, narrow trails that led to the homesteads were so rugged that men had to go on foot, leading their horses up the trail.

Such isolation was one—but certainly not the only—factor that contributed to the rise of outlawry in Utah, including the number of Mormons who swelled the ranks among outlaws.

There were other factors as well. A major factor was the Civil War. As it ended, former soldiers arrived in Utah looking for a fresh place to set down roots. Sadly, a number of those who came arrived in postwar "gangs," still nursing the animosities that had fomented the war to begin with. The influx of these disaffected "outlaws" brought a new breed to the area: men who were trained in guerilla warfare—and who were more than happy to use their "skills" in making their way.

Another major factor was the westward expansion itself and the changing face of the western frontier. As increasing numbers of settlers arrived in the Territory of Utah, as well as in all other corners of the West, conflict erupted. Virtual war broke out among the sheepherders, cattlemen, and sodbusters. Powerful conflicts occurred between those who wanted an open-range policy (with livestock not restricted to a fenced and gated area) and those who preferred a closed-range policy. Even the invention of barbed wire contributed significantly to the rise of outlawry in Utah as cattle rustling among Mormons and non-Mormons alike escalated to precedent-setting levels.

For many, cattle rustling was the "gateway" activity that eventually led to a life of crime—and it's easy to see how it could happen. The Territory of Utah in the mid-nineteenth century was largely a cashless society at first, and cattle meant wealth. Rustling was an "easy" way to get established. As one historian described it: "To obtain a start in the cattle business, young men went out on the desert or into the hills and put their brand on any unmarked animals they found. It was an easy matter to separate a calf from its mother, when it became technically a maverick. Branding calves was a sort of game played by all cattlemen, the winner being the one who got his mark on the largest number."[14] Note the phrase *technically a maverick*: it became a letter-of-the-law versus spirit-of-the-law situation for Mormon boys not previously afoul of the law.

As bullion and currency gradually became standard in the territory, it was logical—and easy—to make the jump from luring calves away from their mothers to luring cash out of the fists that held it, robbing banks, trains, stages, and mines.

Still another factor was a growing "class conflict" between emerging businessmen (some of them Mormons) and the more humble Saints, some of whom were starting to feel oppressed again after walking halfway across the country (and for some, traveling halfway around the world). Large business owners were able to get favorable rates from the railroads, while the struggling small farmers and business owners were forced to pay much higher rates, leading to significant losses in net income. Banks, mines, big businesses, and other enterprises were seen as exploitive and interested in nothing more than growing their wealth and power, even if that meant doing it on the backs of more lowly workers who were desperately trying to better themselves financially. When some chose to fight back against large cattle ranches, big banks, and the prospering railroads by rustling and robbing, they considered it part of a "class struggle" instead of seeing it for the criminal activity it was.

Finally, culture and social attitudes were a powerful factor binding the first- and second-generation Utah Mormons with the outlaws who

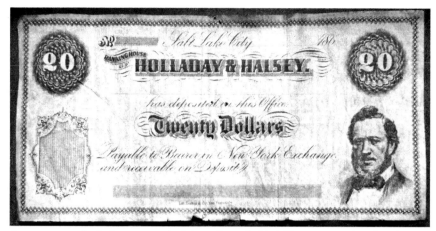

As currency gradually became standard throughout the Utah Territory, it replaced cattle as the mark of wealth, and outlaws went from rustling cattle to robbing banks and trains.

were their neighbors—and who eventually became part of them as some Mormons themselves became outlaws. The set of characteristics the Mormons and outlaws shared later became identified among psychologists and sociologists as the *authoritarian personality syndrome*.[15]

Authoritarian attitudes were definitely not limited to Mormons—nor did the concept originate with them. In fact, the Church had many characteristics in common with the dominant culture of the United States and especially with its New England origins—but in the case of early Utah, the Church was the ruling body, first of the State of Deseret and later of the Territory of Utah. As mentioned, the governing body of Utah's theocracy drew its authority directly from God through the Church officials. While almost all churches are authoritarian in religious matters, the Utah Mormons recognized Church authority in all economic, business, political, and social life as well and readily submitted to its leaders. One of the characteristics of authoritarian personality is the tendency to stereotype—and the very classification of people as either "Mormon" or "Gentile" is a perfect example of such stereotyping in early Utah. It also became the perfect opportunity for some Church members to assume dominance over another group (the non-Mormons), another telltale sign of authoritarianism and a prominent characteristic among the Mormons-turned-outlaws.

Another strong characteristic of authoritarian attitudes is a sense of persecution. Having been driven from their homes in several states, railed against by mobs, denied protection by the government, expelled from the United States, and forced to flee to an uninhabited desert, the early Mormons certainly had good reason to feel persecuted. And their new home—a hostile and unforgiving desert—likely fed their already healthy sense of persecution. It was, plain and simple, wrenchingly difficult to eke out an existence in the new environment. As an example, one community banded together and exerted great effort to dig a ditch that would enable them to irrigate their crops. As it turned out, the supposed life-giving water was so alkaline that it killed all the crops instead.[16] Such experiences actually reinforced earlier feelings of persecution and caused the Mormons to band tightly together, rejecting the outside world and treating outsiders with hostility.

What eventually happened as a result is a situation we don't often associate with members of the Church: in their own small territory, the Mormons became a strong and united "in-group" that exercised great prejudice and hostility to people they considered "outsiders." It's a completely understandable reaction, given what they had suffered and the fact that they had lost everything—more than once—to societies that banded against them. When federal officers started arriving on the scene and threatening to wrest control away from the Church, the Mormons became even more devoted to their Church leaders, who also served as their government leaders. Along with such a mentality

In an effort to help protect themselves from Indians and outlaws alike, early settlers built their homes in walls around forts, as shown in this early Southern Utah settlement. Such an arrangement gave them power in numbers and the protection of those guarding the fort.

came an increasing willingness to attack people who seemed vulnerable or weak or those who were socially acceptable as "victims."[17] And the Mormons, typical of an authoritarian attitude, were out to "prove" something—to prove that their way of life and their religion were the undisputed truth . . . and that no one had the right to challenge them or deny their ability to practice that religion.

Here's where things get interesting: The "outlaws" shared the exact same attitudes and culture. They stereotyped everyone around them—in their view, there were the "outlaws" and the "others." They became in their own sight a strong and united "in-group" that exercised prejudice and hostility against outsiders. Like the Mormons, they clung to power—except in their case, the power wasn't a Church authority, but a gun. For the outlaw, persecution was a daily fact of life; it was almost a full-time job to escape capture and incarceration (or, perhaps worse, conflict with rival gangs of outlaws). As is obvious, they were also willing to attack people who seemed vulnerable or weak or were socially acceptable as victims—in fact, that's how they made their living. Finally, they too were out to "prove" something—toughness, power, strength, and a disdain of the law, qualities that seemed resilient on the surface but that actually covered up intense inhibition and fear.[18]

And there you have it: the similarity between both groups made it simple to slide from one to the other—or to belong to both. Estimates are that about a third of the outlaws in Utah were also Mormons (or had been born into Mormon families). It has been argued, in fact, that tendencies toward outlawry may have been buried in the Mormon culture of the day—and that the opportunities to make the leap were plentiful.

There was an undeniable "subgroup" that existed at the intersection of the Mormon community and the outlaw community: Its members have gone down in history as the fascinating group of Mormon outlaws, some of whom will be examined in this book. As mesmerizing as they are to us, looking back from our far-removed vantage point, they were limited in both time and space.

Why?

A number of factors led to their demise. Improved communication and transportation throughout the West made it much more difficult for outlaws to escape capture; increasing numbers of outlaws were featured on "Wanted" posters and thrown unceremoniously behind bars.

But that's not all. Utah was given statehood, and with it came the return of the Mormon community as a whole to the broader American society—a society that, as the nineteenth century drew to a close, shunned the criminal element, including the outlaws of the Wild West. For Utah's Mormons, the passage of statehood brought the abandonment of their "in-group" identification and a desire instead to embrace the Americanism of the Church's New England roots and societal ways of living. With Utah's status as a state came the move by many of the surviving outlaws to abandon their way of life and settle instead into a peaceful existence that attracted no attention and the opportunity to make an honest living.

Ultimately, Utah's Mormon outlaws vanished. Today, they're the stuff of history books. But the Church that shared their compelling stories continues on, having transcended time, space, and all the lawmen in between.

CHAPTER TWO
Hideouts along the Outlaw Trail

As the latter half of the nineteenth century wore on, the Utah Territory had some unique things to offer the outlaws who did business there—and even those from elsewhere who used the Territory as a resting place from a hectic schedule of rustling cattle, robbing banks, and holding up trains. The first, as discussed in chapter 1, was a culture that practically aided and abetted the outlaws, even contributing members of the local population to their numbers. The other was a terrain that created three of the best hideouts in the nation—hideouts that became the stuff of legend along what became known as the Outlaw Trail.

The Mormon pioneers who arrived in the Salt Lake Valley in July 1847 plodded across prairies and through flatlands before encountering the majestic Rockies with their soaring summits and sheer canyon walls. Finally descending along a precipitous ridge, they reached their eventual destination: a flat and arid valley floor positioned between lakes on the north and south and sandwiched between mountains on the east and west. A river that sliced through the desert floor between the salt-water lake on the north and the fresh-water lake on the south provided the water that sustained life.

Scarcely stopping long enough to catch their breath, the Saints immediately began the arduous task of creating a livable space in a valley wild with grasses and dotted with sagebrush. But until Mormon immigrants began arriving in numbers that necessitated expansion beyond the valley, many locals were unaware of the stunning diversity that comprised the entire Utah Territory landscape.

Winding down the center of the Territory like a giant strand of pearls were the tractable valleys that beckoned to weary travelers and became the mainstay of Mormon settlements. Surrounded and protected by soaring peaks, they offered flat expanses perfect for homes, farms, and fields. Nearby rivers and streams provided irrigation water, and the relative ease of establishing trails kept one settlement connected to the others.

In contrast to the inviting nature of the pristine valleys, much of the rest of the Utah Territory proved inhospitable indeed—at least to the Mormon settlers, who gave a wide berth to the rugged slopes, steep canyons, plunging ravines, and craggy formations of the Territory's red-rock landscape. But those were the *settlers*. What was a curse to them was a blessing to another segment of the population: the outlaws who wanted anything but hospitality and easy access.

And so it was that the legendary Outlaw Trail wound along the eastern edge of the Territory and relied on three ingenious hideouts, each separated by a distance of about two hundred miles as the crow flies. On the top end—located in present-day south-central Wyoming about forty miles southwest of Kaycee, Wyoming—was the Hole-in-the-Wall. In the middle was Brown's Hole, situated in the northeastern section of present-day Utah twenty-five miles downstream from Flaming Gorge. And at the far end, sandwiched between three rivers in present-day southeastern Utah, was Robbers' Roost, beginning at present-day Hanksville. All three—situated solidly in Mormon territory—served as efficient shelters for outlaws from throughout the nation who relied on the rugged landscape for refuge from law enforcement. And all three were home to some of the most exciting and captivating action in the Territory.

The Hole-in-the-Wall

The primitive and remote hideout known as Hole-in-the-Wall was situated in the Big Horn Mountains in present-day south-central Wyoming. It was, in very fact, a literal hole in the wall. The "wall" was a fifty-mile-long red sandstone escarpment known as the "Red Wall." The "hole" was the only break in the entire fifty-mile wall, a narrow V-shaped opening that led through the wall and beyond the mesa into a rich, verdant valley complete with irrigated creek beds—perfect for grazing rustled cattle or stolen horses. Even at its best, it was at least a day's journey from any semblance of civilization.

Part of the fifty-mile-long red sandstone "wall" that stood between the Hole-in-the-Wall and the rest of civilization. The "hole," a narrow V-shaped opening, was the only break in the entire fifty-mile wall and led to the verdant valley on the other side.

It was so isolated, in fact, that when a murder occurred there in 1886—far beyond the pale of the ordinary cattle rustlers and horse thieves—it took more than three days for the dispatched horseman to return with a sheriff.

That isolation made it the perfect hideout for outlaws. Remote and secluded, its narrow pass was stunningly easy to defend; it was impossible for a lawman to approach without alerting the outlaw who guarded the "hole." That's not all: Outlaws who made the steep climb over loose rock at the top of the wall enjoyed a 360-degree panoramic view of the entire area, making it easy to spot any approaching trouble. Posses of lawmen made periodic attempts to enter the hideout, but all were scattered and sent packing by the outlaws who ferociously guarded the entrance.

In its more than fifty years of active existence, no lawman ever successfully entered the area to capture an outlaw. And while several groups of lawmen attempted to infiltrate the area using undercover techniques, none was ever successful.

It may have been isolated, but at its height it wasn't forsaken or abandoned. Quite the opposite: through the hole and on the other side of the wall was the Willow Creek Ranch, boasting six log cabins, a livery stable, a corral, and supplies for large numbers of livestock. (Remains of the cabins can be found in the area today, a spot that is still

The Willow Creek Ranch house at the Hole-in-the-Wall was often used by Butch Cassidy while hiding out there. The outlaws held themselves to a strict code of conduct while at the hideouts along the Outlaw Trail.

very difficult to access. One of the cabins used by Butch Cassidy has been relocated to a museum in Cody, Wyoming, where it is on display to the public.)

The Hole-in-the-Wall was actually used as a hideout by several outlaw gangs, all of whom used the area as a type of "headquarters." They may have shared hideout real estate, but they operated independently, carrying out unrelated, separate robberies with very little interaction. Each of the gangs contributed to the upkeep of the ranch. Members of these gangs rarely if ever saw each other outside the hole, intermingling only when hiding out. And the absentee ranch owners left the outlaws who squatted on their property completely alone; after all, they didn't want to invite any trouble.

The outlaws who sought shelter there may have thumbed their noses at the law, but they actually operated under a definite set of rules. (Who says there is no honor among thieves?) There were specific rules about how to settle disputes and hard-and-fast rules that prohibited stealing from another gang. Codes of behavior helped keep even the outlaws in line. There was no central leader that kept order in the Hole-in-the-Wall; instead, each gang followed its own specific chain of command, but follow they did.

Those gangs included some of the best-known and most infamous outlaws in the nation's history. Most prominent was the Hole-in-the-

The infamous Harvey Logan—better known as "Kid Curry"—was one of the best-known members of the Wild Bunch and spent a lot of time at the Hole-in-the-Wall with many of the Mormon outlaws.

Wall gang, a group of outlaws who took on the name of the hideout and that included Butch Cassidy's Wild Bunch gang as well as outlaws like Kid Curry (Harvey Logan), Black Jack Ketchum, George "Flat Nose" Curry, Elza Lay, and "Laughing" Sam Carey. Outlaws from outside the Utah Territory took advantage of the Hole-in-the-Wall as well, including the Logan brothers and Jesse James.

A steady stream of outlaws used the hideout beginning in the late 1860s; by the end of the nineteenth century, however, very few were using the area—a fact that correlated with the gradual demise of outlaws in the area. Eventually, use of the hideout faded altogether. Even during its heyday, it was not as heavily used as the other two hideouts on the Outlaw Trail—Brown's Hole and Robbers' Roost.

Brown's Hole

Brown's Hole was a valley about forty miles long and ten miles wide; it lay about half-and-half in present-day Utah and present-day Colorado, with the far northern extremity creeping into present-day Wyoming. Stretched along the Green River in northeastern Utah, it is bounded by Cold Spring Mountain on the north and Diamond Mountain on the south. Early explorer Major John Wesley Powell described it this way on his first trip through the area:

> Halfway down the valley, a spur of red mountain stretches across the river, which cuts a canyon through it. Here the walls

are comparatively low, but vertical. A vast number of swallows have built their adobe houses on the face of the cliffs. . . . The young birds stretch their little heads on naked necks through the doorways of their mud houses, clamoring for food. They are noisy people. We call this Swallow Canyon.[19]

The word *hole* was used by nineteenth-century mountain men to describe a valley or basin. But where the name *Brown* came from is a matter of real controversy. Major John Wesley Powell said the place was named after an old-time trapper who built a cabin in the area and used it as a place to hunt deer and trap beavers. A similar theory is that the hole was named after a trapper named Brown who came to hunt one fall and, as a result of heavy snowfall, was confined there until the next spring. One of the earliest legends, dating from 1839, is that a white man named Brown was murdered there by Indians.

Other possible Browns included a character nicknamed "Old Cut Rocks" Brown, a Green River trapper named Charles Brown, and an outlaw named Henry "Bo'sun" Brown. All three apparently inhabited the hole during at least part of its glory days. Ann Bassett, the first white child born in Brown's Hole, claims it was named after a French Canadian trapper with the nickname of Bible-back Brown, who recommended the spot as a great place to find shelter for the winter.

A panoramic view of one of the entrances to Brown's Hole; the geographic features of the basin made it the perfect hideout for outlaws, and its sheer cliffs and mountainous terrain discouraged regular homesteaders and ranchers from settling there.

Several stories owe their origins to some iteration of a French Canadian trapper who first settled the area. In one, a man named Baptiste Brown wandered into the hole and decided to settle down; legend has it that he there built a cabin for himself and his Blackfoot squaw.[20] Another story says that Baptiste Brown is a man who participated in the last battle on the nearby Little Snake River between trappers and Indians. In still another version of the story, Baptiste Brown is actually an alias for French Canadian trapper Jean-Baptiste Chalifoux.

And what do the historians say? University of Wyoming history professor Dick Dunham favors the Baptiste Brown theory; he wrote, "There are no records to prove it: but tradition, passed on from mountain men to early settlers, is so strongly established there seems no reason for doubting it. So to Baptiste Brown we give the credit for being the first white man to settle in . . . the whole intermountain West."[21] Other historians, however, doubt that Baptiste Brown ever even existed; some argue that he was merely a fictional character invented by Colonel Henry Inman in his 1897 book, *The Old Santa Fe Trail*.

An early cattleman who operated out of Brown's Hole, J. S. Hoy, was vehement in his claims that Baptiste Brown never existed, and says that the hole got its name from its physical appearance. The rocks, he wrote, were dark brown, impressing them all "with the same thought—the Hole was rightly named brown." He summed up his account by writing, "All the stories told that it was named after a trapper by the name of Brown are pure fiction."[22]

While there is little agreement about how the hole got its name, everyone agrees that its geographical features made it the perfect hideout for outlaws. The mountainous terrain and sheer cliffs of the area repelled the usual settlers who were looking for a place to homestead and farm; Indians, fur traders, trappers, explorers, and mountain men used the area because of its central location in a rich fur-bearing area. Many of its "residents" were cattle rustlers who took advantage of the natural shelter and mild winters that resulted from the rugged mountains.

Its location made it an ideal "stop-over" where outlaws could rest and regroup before continuing to some other destination. It was tied to the Rocky Mountains on the north by the Oregon Trail and to Santa Fe and other regions of the southwest by the Old Spanish Trail on the south. That's not all: its specific location meant that when state lines

Brown's Hole was an ideal stopover where outlaws could rest and regroup before moving on. Those who did settle in the Hole became friendly with the outlaws, often giving them food and shelter, loaning them money, and warning them when the law approached.

were drawn, the hole found itself sprawled across three states—Utah, Colorado, and Wyoming. An outlaw on the run could avoid capture fairly easily merely by crossing one of the state lines, effectively putting himself out of the jurisdiction of pursuing lawmen.

And while we don't know how Brown's Hole got its name, history is very clear on the first recorded visit by a white man. William Henry Ashley, floating down the Green River in 1825, initially launched above Flaming Gorge. He then rode churning rapids down the river through steep canyons for six days without any food. Suddenly, he wrote, the river widened and the steep canyons drew back; he had entered Brown's Hole. Ten miles below, he recorded, was a "great campground where thousands of Indians had wintered."[23]

During its heyday, almost every mountain man or trapper of any consequence visited Brown's Hole—including Kit Carson, Robert Newell, "Uncle Jack" Robinson, and Joe Meek. While the exact date is uncertain, around 1836 the trappers at Brown's Hole used the idle summer months to build Fort Davy Crockett, which briefly became the economic and social center of the Rocky Mountains for explorers, trappers, and mountain men. Kit Carson was employed there for at least two years as a hunter for the fort, charged with keeping the men supplied with meat.

Rivalry between the hunters and trappers was intense. Licenses were issued by the superintendent of Indian Affairs in St. Louis, granting trading privileges between the trading companies and certain Indian tribes. Apparently the Indians at the fort also ran a brisk business selling dogs for fifteen dollars each to travelers through the area. Obadiah Oakley, who passed through the area on his journey from Illinois to Oregon, found the dog meat "excellent, much better than our domestic beef, and next to buffalo."[24]

Thomas Jefferson Farnham, leader of Oakley's party en route to Oregon, described the fort in these words:

> The Fort is a hollow square of one story log cabins, with roofs and floors of mud, constructed in the same manner as those of Fort William. Around these we found the conical skin lodges of the squaws of the white trappers, who were away on their "fall hunt," and also the lodges of a few Snake Indians, who had preceded their tribe to this, their winter haunt. Here also were the lodges of Mr. Robinson, a trader, who usually stations himself here to traffic with the Indians and white trappers. His skin lodge was his warehouse; and buffalo robes were spread upon the ground and counter, on which he displayed his butcher knives, hatchets, powder, lead, fish-hooks, and whisky. In exchange for these articles, he receives beaver skins from trappers, money from travellers, and horses from the Indians. . . . when all the "independent trappers" are driven by approaching winter into this delightful retreat, and the whole Snake village, two or three thousand strong, impelled by the same necessity, pitch their lodges around the Fort, and the dances and merry makings of a long winter are thoroughly commenced, there is no want for customers.[25]

Others weren't as charitable in their description of the fort. A German traveling through from St. Louis called it "the worst thing of the kind we have seen on our journey," saying that the fort "appeared somewhat poverty-stricken, for which reason it is also known to the trappers as Fort Misery."[26]

Within three years a defining battle took place between a hunting party led by Kit Carson and a band of Sioux Indians that resulted in animosity and activity that would ultimately cause the fort to close.

During the skirmish the Indian chief, attempting a peace-making gesture, was killed by one of the white hunters; in retaliation, a small band of Sioux returned to the fort and stole one hundred and fifty horses. A band of traders from the fort then went on a horse-stealing spree of their own—not from the Sioux, but from friendly forts in the area. A spate of horse-stealing activities then went on over the ensuing dozen years, with leaders at the fort being forced to choose sides. The fractured loyalties split up the partnership of the company running the fort, and all activity at Fort Davy Crockett came to a subsequent halt in 1840—the same year in which major fur trading activities also came to a close, though some fur trading continued for several years beyond that time in Brown's Hole among a handful of white trappers (with a few trapping into the 1870s) and the Ute, Shoshone, and Navajo Indians, who traded pelts for whatever supplies they needed.

Though only minor trading took place, there were lots of other activities at the fort between 1840 and 1843. In November 1842, one traveler through the area said that the days "were given to horse racing, foot racing, shooting matches; and in the evening were heard the music of voice and drum and the sound of dancing. There was also an abundance of reading matter for those inclined in that direction."[27]

The Brown's Hole site of Fort Davey Crockett, at one time the economic and social center of the Rocky Mountains for hunters, trappers, and explorers. While some lauded the fort, its poverty-stricken appearance caused others to call it "Fort Misery."

The ranch of Sam Bassett, an immigrant from upstate New York who was the earliest permanent settler in Brown's Hole. He became one of the most colorful and prominent residents of the Hole and was a great friend to the outlaws who frequented it.

By 1844, the fort had fallen into complete disrepair. Explorer John C. Fremont, traveling through the area, saw only the decrepit remains. There was a fair amount of traffic through the area just after the fort closed, including one group of gold rush hopefuls who wanted to avoid contact with the Mormons in the Salt Lake Valley. A band of Cherokee Indians wintered there in 1849, and a group of Texas cattle ranchers used Brown's Hole as a place to winter their herds en route to California for several years.

The earliest permanent settler—"Uncle Sam" Bassett, who immigrated from upstate New York—apparently staked out his property in Brown's Hole in 1842. A confirmed bachelor, he bemoaned the arrival in 1854 of Warren D. Parsons and his wife, "Snapping Annie," who was expert at driving her oxen. With the arrival of a woman, he wrote in his diary, "Man's freedom in this paradise is doomed."[28]

With the demise of the fur trade, the former trappers and mountain men had to find something else to do, and some inevitably became outlaws. Those who most often used the hole as a hideaway, including Butch Cassidy and his gang, weren't permanent settlers there but simply took advantage of the geographical and cultural features of the spot. Those cultural features included toleration of rivalries, a disregard of economic status, and the free mixing of various racial groups, including Mexicans, Blacks, Indians, and whites. The outlaws were readily accepted as part of the mix; the storekeeper in Brown's Hole occasionally hired outlaws to work in the store and on the ferry without fearing that his property would be compromised. The peculiar set of ethics and mores that developed in the area resulted in a thirty-year period during which the permanent settlers were predominantly cattle rustlers and their main occupation was sheltering outlaws.

The resulting society is fascinating. The permanent citizens were considered "law-abiding rustlers." The transients were considered "outlaws." The cattle rustlers helped themselves to the spoils of the larger cattle companies moving through the area. That was heartily endorsed as a way to build a settler's own herd—until, that is, the locals judged that a herd was large enough. At that point, the settler was expected to stop rustling. The transients supported themselves by robbing banks and railroads. That was also heartily endorsed as a way to make a living—until, that is, a robber had enough. The entire operation on both ends smacked of a Robin Hood mentality: steal from the rich (the huge cattle companies, the banks, the railroads) and give to the poor (the struggling settlers and unemployed transients).

Gradually, the area moved from predominantly cattle rustlers and horse thieves to the kinds of outlaws that committed much more serious offenses. The arrival of Butch Cassidy and his gang catapulted the area

The ruins of the cabin Butch Cassidy built at Brown's Hole.

into a new era. One woman wrote that Brown's Hole (by then often called Brown's Park) had become "a more or less permanent hideout for many who found total honesty a personal encumbrance."[29]

While the youth of both groups liked each other and often mingled, most of the outlaws and the permanent settlers simply avoided each other, sticking to their own business. On the occasions when things did get out of hand, problems were settled amicably. Saloon keepers in the surrounding areas always welcomed the outlaws and let the gunfights erupt unimpeded. Why? The outlaws always came back, paying a dollar for each bullet hole and generously settling any other damages.

And the outlaws felt completely safe there, even from law enforcement. In the first place, very few law enforcement officers dared cross the boundaries into Brown's Hole. Here's how one writer described it:

> A lawman riding into the Hole might just as well stick a gun to his forehead or sleep with a mess of rattlesnakes. Local lawmen weren't cowards. They'd face a bad man in the streets with Colt handguns or Winchester rifles. They'd trail a bad guy across the country and back if need be. But if an outlaw managed to slip into Brown's Hole, no God-fearing lawman, especially if he had a family, was eager to follow.[30]

The few lawmen who did pursue an outlaw into Brown's Hole found that their quarry simply drifted across state lines, just out of legal reach. The permanent settlers willingly harbored outlaws, who often hid out in a cabin in a secluded stand of thick cedars near an established ranch—and the rancher sent riders to warn the outlaws of any approaching lawmen. It appears many of the permanent residents even *liked* the outlaws. Butch Cassidy's sister, Lula Parker Betenson, wrote that Butch "occupied a special place in their hearts. Whenever he worked, he did an honest day's labor for his pay. They trusted him."[31]

A code of ethics gradually became solidified among the people in Brown's Hole, and it applied to everyone from permanent residents to those in the region for a temporary stopover. No stealing or gun slinging was allowed—ever. Women were treated with the utmost respect—without question. You didn't cheat at cards; when a well-known

The view looking back at Brown's Hole from Lodore Canyon, an area where Mormon outlaw David Lant and his partner, Harry Tracy, unsuccessfully tried to escape from pursuing lawmen.

resident was caught dealing off the bottom of the deck, he was knifed and buried just outside the door so the rest could get on with the game. All personal property was respected—without exception. If you wanted a horse or a cow, you bought it, traded for it, or exchanged it for something of equal value. If you took it without permission, you'd be hanged. Just like that. What you did on "the outside" was your own business, and no questions were asked. But while you were in Brown's Hole, you were expected to abide by the established rules. Rancher Charlie Crouse, a permanent resident who hosted many an outlaw in his day, once fatally shot a visitor who crossed the line of propriety and buried him under a pile of rocks to serve as a warning to others.

The permanent residents and the outlaws got along famously, mostly due to the fact that the outlaws came from honest, hard-working folks and related well to the mostly honest, hard-working residents. The outlaws didn't put on airs, and the residents liked that. It was customary for the permanent residents to feed the outlaws as they passed through. In exchange the outlaws did chores, helped around the ranch, or guarded livestock. The irony was rich: Some of the most trusted guards were those who rustled cattle and stole horses when they weren't in Brown's Hole.

The permanent residents and the outlaws even did plenty of business. After all, outlaws brought loads of cash into an area where resources were often scarce. If an outlaw temporarily got down on his luck, he could always find residents who were happy to loan him money—because the outlaws always paid back the loans, often very generously. Residents were also happy to buy horses and cows from the outlaws, even when it was obvious the livestock was stolen—because the outlaws always sold at a price well below market value. Many a Brown's Hole resident built up respectable herds that way. Some of the outlaws even went into business with residents as silent partners, providing solid assets to farms and ranches. And in the ultimate bond of trust, some residents even "adopted" outlaws, giving them a lasting branch on the family tree while turning a blind eye to questionable or downright criminal activities on the outside.

A number of well-known outlaw gangs periodically called Brown's Hole home. And gradually, civilization of a sort came to Brown's Hole. In 1878, Herb and Elizabeth Bassett moved to Brown's Hole and took up residence with Herb's uncle, Sam Bassett, until they could build a cabin of their own. That winter, Elizabeth gave birth to Ann, the first white baby born in the Hole; they eventually established a warm, inviting home that sheltered many who were passing through.

Herb was a quiet, intellectual man who loved to read and play music and who left the ranching up to his wife; his collection of books eventually formed the first public library in the region. Butch Cassidy was one of his most regular patrons; he reportedly spent many hours relaxing in Herb's library with his nose in a book. Herb eventually accepted a job as the local justice of the peace and had to look the other way more often than not when it came to his wife.

As for Elizabeth, she was a fiercely independent, stubborn, well-educated woman who not only ran the ranch but also adopted many feminist causes (including voting rights for women); it was said she could out-rustle, out-shoot, and out-lasso most men. When the local doctor died (the first death by natural causes in the Hole), Elizabeth read his medical books, learned the trade, and took over his practice. Many of the outlaws bragged that they'd be willing to lay down their lives for her if she merely asked. In time, she commanded her own gang of outlaws, the Bassett Gang; legend has it that she pursued an unarmed group of Texans who had earlier shot one of Elizabeth's gang members, personally put the nooses around their necks, and supervised their burial in a shallow, unmarked, common grave in nearby Irish Canyon.[32]

Populated at least to some degree until about 1910 and used by outlaws until the turn of the twentieth century, Brown's Hole was likely the last of the major outlaw retreats in the West. Many of the cabins—including one belonging to Matt Warner, "the Mormon Kid"—are still standing in the area, though the remains are understandably weathered. And providing silent testimony to the life that once ricocheted off the steep canyon walls are clusters of graves that still dot the desolate landscape.

Robbers' Roost

Located in present-day southeastern Utah and tucked between the Colorado River, Green River, and Dirty Devil River, Robbers' Roost is a savage stretch of land characterized by hidden ravines, steep-walled canyons, intricate mazes, myriad caves, countless lookout points, hundreds of hiding places, and extreme heat (part of it crosses the inhospitable San Rafael Desert). A desolate area sandwiched between the Henry Mountains on the west and the La Sal Mountains on the east, with one corner beginning at modern-day Hanksville, the Roost itself had areas lush with grasses that were fed by natural springs.

The southernmost of the hideouts along the Outlaw Trail, Robbers' Roost served some of the most notorious gangs in western history for more than thirty years and was never successfully penetrated by a lawman during those three-plus decades.[33] Butch Cassidy and his Wild Bunch gang of cattle rustlers, horse thieves, train holdup men, and bank robbers considered it the ideal hideout.

Historians may be at odds on how Brown's Hole received its name but are in fixed agreement on how Robbers' Roost got its moniker. It gained both the name and the reputation from being headquarters for the notorious horse thief, Cap Brown. Brown is reputed to have drifted into the high desert country at Robbers' Roost, establishing it as his base of operations sometime in the 1870s. He made a living first by capturing stray horses; later he raided herds, stealing the horses and supplying them to the mining communities in Colorado, primarily Telluride. It was reputed that no herds in the Utah Territory were safe once Cap Brown became aware of them.

After stealing any number of horses, Brown usually took them to the twisted maze of canyons that would become Robbers' Roost in

The trail leading to Robbers' Roost; outlaws with fresh horses and a good head start were able to pound across this territory and then get literally lost in the craggy landscape of the Roost.

order to rest and recuperate. Other times he hired local ranchers to keep the stolen horses on their property for a few days then help him drive them into his hideout at the Roost. The impoverished ranchers always eagerly provided the help because Brown always paid them generously with cash, a commodity that was tough to come up with in those days. The rivers that bounded the Roost and the springs that were found in the canyons provided the critically needed watering holes. Brown would then drive the stolen horses to one of the mining companies in Colorado, where he received handsome wages for the animals.

Evidence suggests that at first he worked alone. Later, finding that the demand from the mining companies far exceeded his ability to secure enough horses on his own, he did what seems second nature for businesses today: he franchised. He took great care in gradually recruiting small groups of young cowboys to help in stealing the horses. One of his young recruits was Butch Cassidy, who later regularly used Robbers' Roost as the headquarters for his Wild Bunch gang (and the cattle they rustled) beginning in the early 1880s.

But Brown wasn't the first horse thief to use Robbers' Roost as a hideout. Two earlier horse thieves, John Griffith and James Howells, were apparently the first to discover the area and to use it as a place to hide their stolen livestock. The two were actually celebrated by unusual nicknames. John Griffith, who had one brown eye and one blue eye, was called "Blue John" because his single blue eye, a deep azure, was his most distinguishing feature. He was further known for his thick British accent and his lone set of threadbare clothing, always in need of laundering. His partner in crime, Smoky Mountains native James Howells, was called "Silvertip" because his grizzled beard resembled the hair of a silvertip grizzly.

According to legend, Blue John and Silvertip went on a spirited crime spree in Moab and barely managed to escape the law. But the sheriff was determined and pursued the pair into the no-man's-land south and west of Moab. As luck would have it, the two disappeared into the maze of natural fortresses that would become known as Robbers' Roost and were able to successfully evade the sheriff. Blue John was so enamored by the area that he used the only wood available in the Roost, mountain cedar, to build a carefully constructed cabin near a large spring. (The cabin and spring—known as Blue John's Cabin and Blue John's Spring—can still be seen today.) The pair continued to use the Roost as a spot to hide the horses they stole until they were able to liquidate them on the market.

Nature and geography made Robbers' Roost the ideal hideout. The only real access was—and still is—a narrow area at the mouth of Dirty Devil River. The natural fortresses, caves, and tunnels in the area provided perfect places for storing caches of weapons and for concealing numberless outlaws and their ill-gotten gains.

Despite random attempts, lawmen were never able to penetrate Robbers' Roost. After a while, no one even tried—it had gained a fierce reputation as being impregnable, and colorful legends added to the intrigue that kept officials at bay. The geography itself is one reason the place was difficult to get into; the residents themselves undoubtedly served as effective deterrents as well. And we'll never know exactly what kinds of defenses were set up, but just the rumors about them would have been powerful disincentives for any lawman who merely *thought* about penetrating the roost.

One small-time outlaw who apparently wanted to be part of Butch Cassidy's Wild Bunch landed in prison and used his time there to write Utah's first governor, Heber M. Wells, about the measures taken by outlaws to protect their turf. He claimed that Robbers' Roost featured an intricate system of tunnels, land mines, and fortifications and was stocked with a vast storehouse of supplies and ammunition—all guarded by a well-armed gang of more than two hundred men. No one knew for sure whether his claims were true, but no one was eager to find out, either.

As time went on, Robbers' Roost housed not only horse thieves but cattle rustlers. The cattle rustlers were actually very sly. Most Utah cattle ranches were much smaller than those in surrounding areas; as the Mormons expanded to more outlying areas of the Territory, the land best supplied by irrigation water had already been taken by farmers. As a result, the cattle ranchers were forced onto much more arid land and therefore were compelled to keep much smaller herds. So instead of making off with a large number of cattle from any one rancher, the rustlers took just a small percentage of each herd—such small numbers, in fact, that the ranchers often didn't even notice any cattle were missing. Even those who did notice figured it wasn't worth the bother to try to track down and recover a few head. It was a sweet deal: Take a few here, take a few there, supplement the numbers with a few mavericks or wild cattle, and soon the rustler had a respectable-sized herd he could take to market. And here's the astonishing irony: The rustlers often paid the very ranchers from whom they stole the cattle to drive them into the Roost.

Utah governor Heber M. Wells was once warned that Robbers' Roost was guarded by more than two hundred men armed with a vast supply of ammunition.

The cattle were usually kept in the Roost only as long as it took pursuing ranchers or lawmen to give up the pursuit. The outlaws knew where the water and grasses were in the Roost; they branded the cattle and kept them thriving as long as it took to move the herds elsewhere. Most often, the rustlers moved the cattle to the Henry Mountains to finish fattening them up for market—sometimes in Price or Green River, but most often in Wyoming or Colorado, where it was less likely the cattle would be identified as stolen.

Ultimately, Robbers' Roost became home to a different brand of robbers: bank robbers and train holdup men. Butch Cassidy and the men who would eventually make up the Wild Bunch became known for their daring robberies—making them notorious to some and folk heroes to others—and they most often cooled their heels in Robbers' Roost after their gallant escapes and before pulling their next big heist.

Because they used the hideout so often, Butch Cassidy and his men tried to imbue it with the comforts of home. Instead of staying in the numerous caves that were found throughout the Roost, they hauled in large canvas tents that they furnished with cozy items. They brought in wagons full of food and drink and invited various women as well— some wives, some sweethearts, and some, known as "camp followers," who were simply enamored with the rugged and daring outlaws. One pair of camp followers became particularly useful to Butch and his gang; they were used as couriers to haul in flour, beans, whisky, and huge loads of ammunition. On one such trip, the pair carried in more than nine hundred pounds of rifle and pistol ammunition.

A motley combination of horse thieves, cattle rustlers, and bank robbers continued to use the Roost until about the end of the nineteenth century. The different groups essentially tolerated each other and for the most part left each other alone. But there were some things even

The natural landscape of Robbers' Roost was so formidable that few lawmen ever attempted to penetrate it. Despite the blistering heat in the summer months, it served as a hideout for many of the outlaws from throughout the West.

the rough-and-tumble outlaws in the Roost wouldn't tolerate—and that included sheep. Most groups had a sheep or two to supply wool, but an entire flock of sheep was simply out of the question; for one thing, they didn't bring in nearly the bounty that cattle and horses did. For another thing, sheep gnawed the grass clear to its roots and left no grazing materials for the more lucrative livestock. So when the Snow brothers from Utah County showed up with a massive flock of sheep, the outlaws leveled a serious ultimatum: clear out by this time tomorrow, or we'll hang you and shoot all your sheep. Needless to say, the hapless Snow brothers (called "scum" and "white trash" by the outlaws) promptly cleared out their sheep (which the outlaws called "range maggots").[34]

Once Butch Cassidy and his partner, Harry Longabaugh (better known as the Sundance Kid), left for parts south—South America, to be exact—in 1902, the Roost became largely abandoned. A final surge of criminal activity went on there during the Prohibition era, when a number of illegal whisky stills were built at the springs that populated the canyons, safe from the prying eyes of sheriffs and other lawmen intent on stopping the manufacture of moonshine. History hasn't preserved the names or stories of those who produced alcohol during the Depression, but the ruins of the illegal stills remain today.

Those aren't the only evidences we still have of what went on in Robbers' Roost more than a hundred years ago. Visitors to the area today can still see the Wild Bunch corral, a couple of cabins, a stone chimney, and several carvings made by outlaws determined to preserve their history.

Much more recently, the Robbers' Roost area gained international fame: In April 2003, hiker Aron Ralston, exploring the area by himself, became trapped when his right hand was crushed by an eight-hundred-pound boulder. When he was unable to move the boulder, Ralston amputated his own hand, applied a makeshift tourniquet, and rappelled out of the canyon, where he was eventually found by a rescue helicopter. His story was subsequently featured in books and movies that emphasized the rugged and remote terrain of the Robbers' Roost area.

Mug shot of Butch Cassidy—Robert LeRoy Parker—at the age of twenty-seven as he entered the Wyoming State Penitentiary on July 15, 1894. The hair combed down over his forehead hides the scar left by a bullet during a shootout with Deputy Sheriff Bob Calverly.

CHAPTER THREE
Butch Cassidy

THE FIRST TIME ANYONE HEARS it, the reaction is almost always the same.

"*What?* Butch Cassidy was a *Mormon?*"

He's pretty much larger than life, unarguably Utah's most famous outlaw. He's the stuff of legend and the fodder of folklore. Known as "the Robin Hood of the West," he took from the rich and gave to the poor and defended the down-and-out. He negotiated life with a gun in his hand but preached against violence. During the last few decades of the nineteenth century, he lined his pockets with millions of dollars in today's cash equivalent during a string of daring bank and train robberies. Cementing his place in the outlaw hall of fame, he was splashed across the silver screen by Hollywood producers, brought to life by a ruggedly handsome Paul Newman.

And yes, he was a Mormon.

Born Robert LeRoy Parker on April 15, 1866, in Beaver, Utah, Butch was the oldest child born to devout Mormons who both emigrated across the plains to the Salt Lake Valley. Both parents were enormously devoted to their religious faith.

These were hardy souls who came from hardy stock.[35] Butch's paternal grandparents, Robert and Ann Parker, were some of the earliest converts to the Church in England. When twenty-year-old Robert's family disowned him for joining the Church, he moved into the mission home and helped attract investigators by singing hymns on street corners where the missionaries preached. When Robert invited Ann Hartley—a coworker from the textile factory where he was a weaver—to one of the street meetings, she too embraced the gospel. The two were married and presided over the mission home, where Ann used her cooking and homemaking skills to care for the missionaries. Of their six children born in England, two young girls died before the family embarked on their long journey to Utah.

As it turned out, their departure was actually hastened by Butch's father, Maximilian. As a young child, his job was to polish the shoes of the missionaries, a task he strongly disliked. So Robert arranged for Maxi, then only nine, to apprentice in the textile mill—a situation he also intensely disliked. Much to the family's disgrace, he ran away from the mill, unceremoniously dumping his responsibilities; even after being severely punished for his misdeed, he refused to return to his duties there. Embarrassed, the Parkers sped up their departure. They sold their home and possessions at a loss and boarded the *Enoch Train* at Liverpool along with more than five hundred other Saints. They subsequently traveled by train from New York City to Iowa City.

The Parkers loaded a handcart and set out for Utah with 221 other people on June 11, 1856, in the Daniel D. MacArthur Company, the second of the handcart companies to leave Iowa. Robert pulled; twelve-year-old Maxi helped his mother push. Ten-year-old Martha Alice walked with six-year-old Arthur; the baby, Ada, was tucked into the handcart with the family's meager supplies.

Just beyond Winter Quarters, Robert's feet became so infected that he had to ride the rest of the way in one of the wagons, leaving Ann and Maxi to pull their handcart on their own. The brutal conditions—including backbreaking labor, poor diet, and relentless sun—so changed Ann's physical appearance that at one point she didn't recognize her own reflection in a pool of water. Finally, about fifty miles from the Salt Lake Valley, she simply sunk to the ground in exhaustion; according to one account, she pushed their handcart over a cliff. That night a passing carriage driver lifted Ann and the four children into the rig and brought them into the valley. They arrived on September 27, 1856, a day behind the rest of the company.

The Parkers moved first to American Fork and then to Beaver, where the family lived in a dugout the first winter and Robert found employment in a woolen mill. That spring Robert built a cabin, which housed his family—including the three additional children who were later born in Beaver. (One of those children, the only boy, died at thirteen months.) Nine years later the family moved to Washington, near St. George, where Robert worked in the cotton and silk mill and served as postmaster.

Entering plural marriage by taking a second wife, he was dogged by federal officials around the state and then throughout his mission to England. He was finally arrested at the age of seventy-one as he left a session of the April 1891 general conference in Salt Lake City. He was held in prison for three days until he posted a $1,000 bond—close to $20,000 in today's currency. Ironically, his second wife worked as a cook for the US Marshal who was instrumental in his arrest.

Robert lived the rest of his days in Washington, Utah, where he died on February 24, 1901, two years after Annie's death. Both are buried in the Washington City Cemetery.

At the age of eighteen, Butch's father, Maxi, traveled back across the plains to St. Louis—not once, but twice—to help groups of Saints make the trek to Utah. When his parents moved to Washington he stayed in Beaver, where he married, fought in the Utah Indian Blackhawk War, and lived a quiet existence for the rest of his days. As a gentle, soft-spoken widower in his nineties, he was often seen on the ground playing marbles with the neighborhood boys and was known for sharing his bountiful garden crop with the widows in town, a habit that earned him the nickname of "the silent giver." He died at the age of ninety-four on July 28, 1938, the oldest man in Piute County.

Butch's mother, Ann Campbell Gillies, was born in Newcastle upon Tyne in northern England, where her family had moved from Scotland shortly before her birth. She was the second of four children. The family joined the Church and left Liverpool on the *Horizon* when Annie was nine. The ship, carrying almost nine hundred members of the Church, was extremely late leaving port—the first in a series of tragic events culminating in its passengers, later members of the Martin and Willie handcart companies and the Hodgetts and Hunt wagon trains, being trapped in bitter winter storms near the Continental Divide in Wyoming. Hundreds lost their lives.

Traveling by train from New York City to Iowa City, the Gillies family rode with hundreds of other Saints in cattle cars, sitting on their luggage. Arriving in Iowa City, families were divided into four groups; two, made up of the more impoverished Saints, would pull handcarts, and two would travel by wagon. Annie's family was able to purchase a wagon—something that undoubtedly contributed to sparing their lives—and was assigned to the Hodgetts Company.

Arriving at Winter Quarters perilously late in the summer, the four companies—comprised of the poorest of the Saints—could not afford to stay the winter there and pressed forward to Salt Lake against the counsel of Church leaders. The Hodgetts Company did not pull out until August 28, facing a journey of more than a thousand miles as winter rapidly approached.

No provisions were available that late in the year when they reached Fort Laramie, so they pressed on with only a fraction of their rations still remaining and half of their journey still ahead. The Hodgetts Company was actually two weeks behind the ill-fated Martin and Willie companies when rescuers finally arrived to bring the freezing and starving immigrants to the Salt Lake Valley. Annie and her family arrived in the valley on November 30, 1856, and are listed as survivors on the Martin's Cove historical marker.

After a short stay in Wood's Cross, north of Salt Lake, the family moved to Beaver. Annie's father, Robert, died at forty-six of pneumonia while traveling back to Woods Cross on business; her mother stayed in Beaver the rest of her life and was active in the Church until her death at the age of eighty-six.

It was this legacy that brought Maxi and Annie together; they met in Beaver and married for time and eternity on Annie's birthday in 1865 in the Endowment House. In large part because of the sacrifices made by their parents in gathering to Zion with the Saints, both were unswervingly dedicated to the Church—and both fully intended on raising a family that had the same devotion. Butch Cassidy, then, wasn't just a Mormon: He was a Mormon boy raised under the pale of two generations of devout pioneers who sacrificed all they had for their faith.

There were certain expectations.

And those expectations, for all intents and purposes, were shattered. (Butch wasn't the only wayward son who caused his mother grief in her waning years; most of the boys in the family followed their father's example as he eventually strayed here and there from the strict covenants that are part of full Church activity.)

Butch was born in his grandmother's stone house and was named Robert LeRoy Parker after his two grandfathers, Robert Parker and Robert Gillies. Records aren't clear on exactly how many children the Parkers eventually had; some say twelve, others thirteen, and a few fourteen. But this much is clear: There were a lot of Parkers, and Butch was the first.

Butch Cassidy wasn't his only alias, and there was a fair amount of confusion later about exactly what his legal name was. His parents called him Roy, and many thought that was his actual name. While in Wyoming as a young man, he started using the alias George; even his file with the Pinkerton's National Detective Agency—an early version of the FBI—claims his legal name was George LeRoy Parker. His next alias was George Cassidy, the last name borrowed from Mike Cassidy, the friend who lured him into a life of crime and who gave him his first gun. From there it was briefly Ed Cassidy, and then a short leap to Butch, a nickname he got while working in a butcher shop in Rock Springs. The only name most folks now remember, actual or alias, is Butch Cassidy.

As was the tradition of the day, his grandfather Robert Parker made the trek from Washington to Beaver to give his new grandson a name and a blessing. Just nine days after Butch was born, his twenty-two-year-old father enlisted in the army and left home to fight in one of the battles of the Blackhawk War.

It wasn't the last time Annie would be left to fend for herself: Quiet and self-assured, Maxi was also the restless sort. He lived and worked out of town most of the time Butch was growing up, and Annie often kept her brood at her mother's house for both help and companionship.

Anyone who drives through Beaver today will see a tranquil, unassuming hamlet, an image that belies the town in which Butch Cassidy spent his first thirteen years. The atmosphere in Beaver back then provides crucial context to how a boy from such a devout family could wander so far off the straight and narrow path.

There's no mistaking it: There was plenty of excitement going on in Beaver, and Butch was a boy who craved excitement. For one thing, Fort Cameron—a military fort that Butch's father helped build on the outskirts of town—included a handful of saloons and everything that went along with them, fueling the imagination of many local boys. That's

Above: Ruins of Fort Cameron on the outskirts of Beaver. Below: Accused Mountain Meadows participant John D. Lee in his coffin. Both the fort and Lee's execution are believed to be influences in Butch Cassidy's decision to abandon his faith and lead the life of an outlaw.

not all: When Butch was eleven, the entire town was obsessed—virtually whipped into a frenzy, really—with the trial of John D. Lee, accused of instigating the killing of a group of immigrants from Arkansas at Mountain Meadows near Cedar City. It was likely the most exciting thing to have happened in Beaver— at least in Butch's lifetime.

Lee was found guilty on March 10, 1877, and was sentenced to death. Justice was rapid in those days; Lee was scheduled to be executed just thirteen days later. More than 275 Beaver residents—the Parker and Gillies families among them—quickly signed a petition asking the governor to pardon Lee; after all, they argued, he was only one of those who had participated in the massacre. Not only that, he was in poor health. A second petition in nearby Panguitch garnered more than five hundred signatures. The governor agreed to the pardon if Lee would confess and name the others involved in the incident. Lee refused and was executed on schedule.

The home in Circleville, Utah, built by Butch Cassidy's father, Maximilian Parker, on a 160-acre ranch. Butch lived there from the age of thirteen until he left home at eighteen.

During his last few years in Beaver, Butch began to drift away from Church activity, even though his mother remained steadfastly faithful; by then, his father was in the habit of missing a few meetings here and there. When Butch continued to come up with one excuse after another to stay home from meetings, eventually his parents gave up trying to make him go.

When Butch was thirteen, his father purchased a 160-acre ranch in the town of Circleville, between Beaver and Panguitch at the confluence of Cottonwood Creek and the Sevier River in present-day southern Piute County, where several friends had already settled. At the time, there were little more than a few stores and a small schoolhouse in town. The two-room cabin that was on the ranch when they bought it is still standing today with the additions Maxi constructed.

Their first few winters in Circleville were the most severe recorded before or since in the area; the extreme cold killed all but two of the family's herd of cattle, and the fierce winds destroyed the entire crop of wheat from the first two spring plantings. It was years before the family recovered financially from their beginnings in Circleville.[36]

Several years later, the family homesteaded fifty acres of adjoining land, building a small cabin on the land to meet the homestead requirements and undergoing backbreaking labor to tame the land with nothing more than a hoe. But through an act of dishonesty, they later lost those fifty acres. While Maxi was working out of town, a local saloonkeeper approached Annie with the proposition that he lease the land for forty dollars so he could build a mill there. Thinking it sounded like a good deal, Annie signed the papers. Only later did the dismayed Maxi and Annie discover that the papers were actually a deed to the land—and Annie had not leased it but sold it.[37]

Though the matter was taken to a Church court, the bishop ruled against the Parkers and allowed the saloonkeeper to keep the fifty acres. Maxi remained convinced that the bishop's ruling was due to one thing: Maxi had temporarily taken up smoking. In actuality, the bishop may have ruled as he did because, in his opinion, Maxi already owned plenty of land. The incident left Maxi feeling badly shaken, and some claim he would have left the Church had it not been for his faithfully devout wife.

Notwithstanding occasional setbacks like those mentioned, the Parker home was a happy one. Everyone had a nickname, ranging from the ridiculous to the sublime; while one of his sisters was called "Cute," Butch was known as "Sally which would lead any boy to be bad."[38] While Butch had stopped going to Church, he willingly participated in the family's weekly "home evening," with its emphasis on doctrinal study; he often played the harmonica while the rest sang hymns. With the ranch isolated from nearby towns, the family had to create its own entertainment; playacting and music often punctuated the air, and Butch occasionally staged grasshopper races. The Parker kids constructed a dam in the Sevier River just south of the ranch and spent hot summer afternoons swimming in the cool mountain runoff.

Compensating for the insecurities of ranching and coping with a growing number of children, money was a constant issue; the Parkers were considered, by any standard, poor. Maxi secured a variety of jobs to supplement the family income, and as the oldest, Butch worked at local ranches to help earn money for the family. He was considered hardworking, solid, and dependable. Rancher Patrick Ryan, who first hired Butch when he was only thirteen, noted that the short, stocky boy could already do the work of a man on the ranch; he described Butch as smart, dependable, quiet, and inoffensive, and was sorry to see him go two years later when he found work a little closer to home.[39]

Despite Ryan's glowing assessment of Butch, it appears that his first scrape with the law happened while he was in Ryan's employ—but it was relatively minor, and certainly far from what he would later commit. In need of new overalls, Butch apparently took some time off from the ranch and went to the nearest town to purchase a pair. Finding the only store in town closed, he mulled over what he should do. Rationalizing that he had taken time off work and had come some distance to purchase the overalls, Butch broke into the store and tried on a variety. Finding the pair he wanted, he left an IOU note for the storekeeper and returned to the ranch. Arriving at the store the next morning, the storekeeper was furious and alerted the authorities. But since Butch had left a note that gave his name, authorities eventually ended up settling the matter outside of court—but not without some drama.

On another occasion, Butch was accused of stealing a saddle, charges that were apparently unfounded. During the time it took to sort the matter out, Butch was held behind bars and was allegedly badly mistreated by authorities—with no subsequent apologies when it was found that he hadn't stolen the saddle after all.

The year he was sixteen, Butch worked at the Marshall ranch nine miles south of the Parker ranch; Annie ended up running the dairy on the ranch and also made and sold cheese and butter to supplement her

Seventeen-year-old Robert LeRoy Parker, just before he assumed the alias Butch Cassidy, on a ranch near Hanksville, Utah.

income, money the family desperately needed. During the next two summers, Annie moved to the same ranch with the rest of the boys so she could avoid the nine-mile trip and get an early enough start on her daily work. The girls stayed behind on the Circleville ranch and cared for their father.

So how did a hard-working, solid, dependable boy like Butch with such devout lineage end up . . . well, where he ended up? Some of the blame may be placed on events Butch experienced either directly or indirectly, including the upset over the overalls, his vicious mistreatment by authorities over the saddle he didn't steal, and the bishop failing to return his father's homestead. Butch interpreted all three incidents with a jaded worldview understandable from his perspective: Justice isn't always exacted as it should be. Some have also wondered if his father's sagging Church activity may have played a small role; all the Parker boys, as mentioned, followed that example. The salacious atmosphere of Beaver may also have started the ball rolling, especially with Butch drifting away from activity in the Church during his time there. But the real homer out of the ballpark was a pair of men Butch worked with—and admired—at the Marshall ranch.

One was Jim Marshall, son of the owner; after being indicted for extortion, he took off and surfaced later at Brown's Hole, where he joined a gang of outlaws. An even greater influence was Mike Cassidy, a two-bit outlaw who somehow got hired on and who took great interest in Butch. As for Butch, by then seventeen, he took an immediate liking to the older, more sophisticated ranch hand and his delightfully shady friends.

Even though Mike was only a few years older than Butch, he was much wiser to the ways of the world and had been on his own far too long, drifting from ranch to ranch and honing his skills as not only an expert horse wrangler but an adept cattle rustler. Mike gave Butch a saddle and a gun and taught him how to shoot. Part of Butch's tutelage that summer at the hands of Mike Cassidy was a course in creative cattle branding: Mike would bring stolen cattle onto the ranch whenever the owner was absent, and he and Butch would wield the iron.

Not particularly wise in the ways of the world, Annie still knew trouble when she saw it, and she knew Butch had definitely fallen in with the wrong element. She could also see that some dubious things were going on and that her oldest son was smack dab in the middle of it all. So even though the family still needed her earnings from the dairy and even though she was pregnant and in no physical shape to launch a full-scale move, Annie gathered up Butch and the other boys and moved back to the Parker ranch in Circleville.

But it was simply too late for now eighteen-year-old Butch. He had no intention of staying on the ranch—or in Utah, for that matter.

Accounts about exactly what happened vary. According to some, Butch was implicated in some cattle rustling. According to others, he accepted the blame for some stolen cattle, even though he was not directly involved. And still others say he stole a couple of horses from a neighboring rancher. (While his family vehemently denied that Butch had stolen horses from a neighbor, Butch himself reportedly admitted it to fellow Mormon outlaw Matt Warner.) Regardless of the precipitating event, the result was the same: Butch approached his mother one June afternoon in 1884 and told her he was leaving home the next morning.

Matt Warner—known as "the Mormon Kid" and later one of Butch's partners in crime—reflected, "Butch Cassidy was a good-natured outlaw. Like me, he turned to the wrong side of the law because of an event that happened when he was a child. At 18, he thought the deputies in his hometown of Circleville was [sic] out to get him for thieving a horse, so he skipped town and fell with the likes of cattle rustlers. . . . He was a smart cuss. If he would have put his mind to it, he could have been and done anything."[40]

Annie's pleas to get Butch to stay fell on deaf ears. She couldn't even get him to wait until the next day, when his father would return home. The ranch, Butch said, was too dull and boring. He felt he had no future there. He was sick of never having a dime to rub between his fingers. He was ready to do the kind of work that would bring him *real* money, and he told her his sights were set on Telluride, Colorado, where plenty of Mormon boys had gone before him to take advantage of the mining boom. He told his mother that he and his friend Eli Elder were headed east to make their fortunes.

Annie rolled up some provisions—including a jar of Butch's favorite preserves—in an old woolen blanket he could tie behind his saddle. He rode off on his mare Babe, towing his colt Cornish to the echo of Annie's voice admonishing him to hurry back.

No one knows exactly where Butch really went, but it wasn't to Telluride—at least not then. And it wasn't with Eli Elder. And he didn't hurry back. Some think he had been hired by notorious horse thief

Cap Brown to drive a herd of stolen horses to Cap's ranch in Brown's Hole, though that's not certain. The best anyone knows is that he drifted from one ranch to another between 1884 and 1886, working as a migrant ranch hand in Utah, Wyoming, Nebraska, and Montana. Evidence indicates that by 1886, he was living under his real name near Meeteetse, Wyoming, where historians have found his signature on a petition for construction of a bridge.

During part of that time he also worked at a butcher shop in Rock Springs, where he took on the nickname of Butch—and in a rumored effort to avoid bringing shame to his honest, hard-working parents, he permanently took on the last name of Cassidy, an obvious nod of affection to his mentor, Mike Cassidy. Fittingly, the butcher shop—owned and operated by Brown's Hole outlaw Charlie Crouse—sold beef from rustled cattle. And what became of Mike Cassidy? He eventually simply disappeared after murdering a Wyoming rancher; he had already left the Marshall ranch—some say for Mexico—by the time Butch left home at eighteen.

In 1886, two years after he galloped away from Annie, Butch showed up in Brown's Hole (by then called "Brown's Park" by many) and took a job with Charlie Crouse racing horses. Ann Bassett, whose family lived in Brown's Hole, described a well-mannered Butch, someone she never saw pack a gun, never knew to be drunk, and never participated in the riotous parties following the horse races. While she knew he was later wanted by the law, she claimed she had no personal knowledge of "any of his deeds of outlawry."[41]

Butch quickly tired of the work at Brown's Hole and moved on—true to his word of two years earlier—to Telluride, where he got a job packing ore from the mines on the backs of mules and taking it down the mountain. While he enjoyed the work, he must have felt that familiar restlessness—and when he met outlaw Matt Warner, it didn't take long for Warner to persuade Butch to abandon the mining gig and become his partner in his horse-racing enterprise. The two ran the racing circuit with Matt's horse, Betty, and never lost a race. (For more information on this part of Butch's life, see chapter 4.)

When the racing circuit got old, Butch and Matt Warner approached affluent rancher Harry Adsit looking for work and claiming their forte was breaking broncos. Adsit kept two thousand horses and five thousand cattle on his twenty thousand-acre ranch near Norwood, Colorado, and saw right away that the pair was expert at riding and breaking horses. He was so impressed, in fact, that he gave the two cowboys one of the rooms in his two-room cabin; he and his wife stayed in the other.

Adsit took an immediate liking to the affable Butch, describing him as someone who "cared not at all for liquor or cards, although he occasionally held the candle while the boys played poker on a saddle blanket in the open." Adsit said Butch often confided his ambitions around the campfire, saying Butch was determined to "make a mark in this world—and he did."[42]

After laboring on the Adsit ranch for a year, Butch told the rancher he wanted to visit his family in Utah. As a show of his affection for the hard-working cowboy, Adsit presented Butch a gift: two of the finest four-year-old horses he had broken. And so it was that Adsit waved his hat in what he believed to be a temporary farewell to Butch, Matt Warner, and Matt's brother-in-law, Tom McCarty.

But Butch didn't saddle up and head toward home—and he had no intention of either visiting family or returning to the ranch. Just two weeks later—in what was to become his graduation "from high-spirited cowboy to full-fledged outlaw"[43]—Butch and his companions instead rode into Telluride. After three days visiting the town saloons and meticulously casing the San Miguel Valley Bank, the three quietly rode up to the bank late on the morning of Monday, June 24, 1889. All three dismounted. Tom stayed outside with the horses. Butch and Matt ambled into the bank and approached the lone cashier. Matt shoved his pistol into the man's face while Butch jumped behind the cage and filled several sacks with currency and gold from the counter and the vault.[44] The take was approximately $21,000—nearly $400,000 in today's currency. Shouting through the door, Tom invited the cashier to stay put and keep quiet or pay with his life.[45] He then shot at the feet of the cashier to motivate him to stay still—a shot that spooked Butch's horse, causing it to buck. Butch wasn't thrown, but his hat flew off his head.

Heady with the rush of committing their first big hit, the three galloped at full speed away from the bank, firing their pistols in random directions to intimidate but not injure passersby on the street. They weren't immediately pursued by law enforcement: Apparently Butch had cut a deal with the town marshal, Jim Clark, who agreed to be out of town during the actual robbery. They left Clark's share of the money in a hollow log outside of town and sped away as fast as they could drive the horses.

They might have succeeded in remaining anonymous, but there was an unanticipated glitch in their carefully laid plans. As they flew out of town, they passed none other than Harry Adsit, who was on his way into town and who recognized Butch and Matt as his ranch hands. When he called out a greeting, Butch yelled, "Haven't got time to talk. Adios!"[46]

Adsit was puzzled. For one thing, Butch wasn't wearing a hat, which was unheard of. For another, Adsit had expected they'd be at least halfway to Utah by then on their way to the purported family visit. It wasn't until he saw an approaching posse in the distance that it occurred to him there might be trouble.

Once the posse caught up to Adsit, the elderly sheriff J. A. Beattie breathlessly asked Adsit if he had seen the trio. Nodding, Adsit asked what they had done and realized that the job was likely planned around the campfire on his own ranch. Thrusting a Winchester at Adsit, the sheriff ordered Adsit to take over and lead the posse.

Adsit continued the pursuit but wasn't intent on catching the cowboys for whom he had developed great affection. At one point the outlaws had stopped for lunch and to saddle up fresh horses when Adsit came upon them. They invited Adsit to join them for lunch, "but the offer was respectfully declined for reasons best known to himself."[47] Adsit then gave the trio plenty of time to gain a head start before starting after them anew. After nearly a forty-mile pursuit, Adsit saw the outlaws riding down the mountain and worried that he was going too fast and might actually catch up to the desperadoes. The sheriff finally ordered Adsit and two others to try to head off the bandits near Rico; that too failed.

By then Adsit had ridden more than a hundred miles and had changed horses three times. He was exhausted, and he demanded a rest. After all, he'd originally been on a leisurely trot toward town, minding his own business, when he had been conscripted into the posse. What must his wife think by now?

The trio was never captured. With Adsit pacing the posse, it was an unlikely scenario in the best of conditions. The bandits eventually made their way down Dolores Canyon to a hideout they had arranged for in advance. Adsit never admitted his relationship to Butch and Matt and refused to reveal Butch's real name. (As it turns out, Butch's brother Dan played a minor role in the robbery, cutting the telegraph wires before the robbery and waiting with one of the sets of relay horses outside town.)

Had the sheriff been more motivated and the bank been better funded, the trio might have been captured after all—and all because of one of the horses Adsit had given Butch when he left the ranch. Ten days after the robbery, Adsit received a letter from Butch: It had come to Butch's attention that the San Miguel County sheriff was riding the dapple brown colt Adsit had given Butch. Butch asked Adsit to recover the horse and send it to him in Moab.

In a burst of civic duty, Adsit showed the sheriff the letter and suggested that he go to Moab to arrest the three bandits. The sheriff refused; he didn't want to make the trip, and neither the county nor the bank had the money to finance it anyway. That's not all: he refused to hand over the horse, declaring his intention to keep it to help cover his expenses for the aborted chase. (As for Adsit, he later bragged that it was his pleasure to pay his own expenses as leader of the posse.)

Butch and Matt separated from Tom and then eventually went their separate ways as well. Butch wintered over in Star Valley, Wyoming, on the Utah border—an area in which he felt safe because the deep snows kept the roads in and out of the area closed for much of the winter. With his native charm and quick wit, Butch established strong friendships with many of the residents of Star Valley, including children, and briefly co-owned a ranch, which he later abandoned. When Butch was arrested for stealing horses from the Pitchfork ranch, he was sentenced to two years in the state penitentiary in Rawlins, Wyoming, and was released six months early for good behavior in 1896.

Once out of jail, Butch got serious about outlawry. Needing the support of accomplices, he assembled a group of bandits that became known as "the Wild Bunch." Of the sixty or so outlaws who comprised the group, roughly a third were also Mormons. Some of the more notorious outlaws included Harry Longabaugh, famous as "the Sundance Kid"; Ben Kilpatrick, known as "the Tall Texan"; Harvey Logan, with the alias of "Kid Curry"; and Butch's best friend, Elza Lay. Under Butch's leadership, they carried off the longest sequence of successful bank robberies and train holdups in the history of the American West.

The Parker family in 1895 when Butch was in prison in Wyoming. *From left:* Leona, Mark (on horse), Eb, Joe Rawlins (in buggy), Lula (with blurred face), Annie, Nina, and Sue Knell. *(Brigham Young University, G. E. Anderson collection)*

The Parker family, 1895; this photograph was taken while Butch was incarcerated in the state penitentiary at Rawlins, Wyoming.

Mysteries and uncertainties about Butch and his career abound, but one thing is sure: Butch Cassidy deserved his reputation as a gentleman bandit; as best as anyone can tell, he never killed anyone, not even during the commission of his crimes and not even in self-defense. Even while living in the roughest possible outlaw hideouts, he insisted that others be treated with respect and would not tolerate the presence of prostitutes.

Perhaps in his own convoluted version of the Golden Rule, he apparently also deserved his widespread reputation as a Robin Hood. Sixteen-year-old Harry Ogden from Escalante spent his life's savings on the best horse he could afford and a sixty-dollar saddle; while Ogden was riding along the edge of Robbers' Roost one afternoon in 1898, an outlaw forced him off his mount, gave Ogden a swift kick in the pants, and rode off on his horse. Three weeks later, Butch Cassidy showed up at Ogden's door along with the outlaw, still on Harry's horse. When Harry identified his horse and the outlaw who had stolen it, Butch ordered the outlaw to start walking—and declared there was no room in that country for a man who would mistreat a young boy.

Another time, a farmer Butch loved faced foreclosure on his land. Butch went to the bank, paid the farmer's mortgage, and delivered

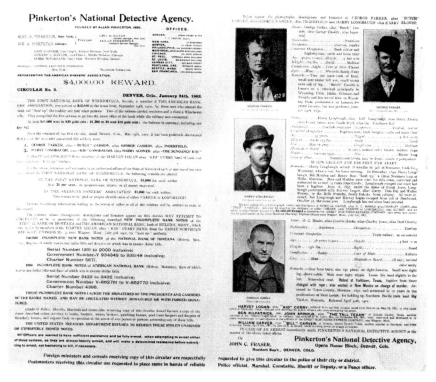

Widely distributed "wanted" poster for Butch Cassidy and the Wild Bunch sponsored by Pinkerton's National Detective Agency.

the deed to the grateful and surprised farmer and his wife. The next day Butch returned to the bank and robbed it for the amount of the mortgage, getting his money back.

And on yet another occasion, Butch began to attack a lone rider in an isolated stretch of land, believing him to be a lawman. When the terrified man explained that he was not a sheriff but a priest, Butch rapidly apologized and asked what on earth the man of the cloth was doing in such a remote area. When it became obvious that the priest had gotten lost, Butch, acting as a guide, accompanied him to his intended destination. That's not all: He offered the clergyman a sizable wad of money as a donation to his church. (By then, the priest easily deduced how the money had been obtained and rejected the generous contribution.)

And while Butch's career is shrouded in myth, there's one thing upon which all the historians agree: He owed his success to three things. One was his meticulous planning; if there was one thing Butch was better at than any of the other outlaws in the nineteenth-century American West, it was planning a robbery. His very first bank robbery stands as convincing evidence: Even after all the hours spent around the campfire on Harry Adsit's ranch planning the San Miguel Valley Bank heist, Butch and his two partners took their sweet time once they arrived in Telluride, spending three days carefully casing the bank and studying the best way to pull off the job. Other times they camped in the area of intended marks for as long as two weeks, watching the habits of the locals.

The second thing Butch had nailed down was something unique to his capers. Simply stated, he disabled communication. In a day when settlements in the West were separated by miles of unfriendly terrain, Butch had a silent, unseen partner cut the telegraph wires down the

Some members of the Wild Bunch: seated, L to R, Harry Longabaugh (the Sundance Kid), Ben Kilpatrick, Butch Cassidy; standing, L to R, Bill Carver, Harvey Logan (Kid Curry).

road at just about the exact moment each robbery took place. The result? Local lawmen could respond fairly quickly but couldn't send for backups—or alert officials in the direction of the outlaws' getaway. Butch and his Wild Bunch generally had a hefty head start before officials at any distance even got word of the robbery.

Finally, Butch perfected the relay concept. It was simple: Before any robbery, he posted teams of relief horses tucked out of sight along the planned getaway route, complete with trusted fellow outlaws to guard, feed, and water the fresh animals. As he and his companions raced away from the scene of the crime on the fastest short-distance runners they could find, they went full throttle, knowing there were relief animals not far away. The two or three or more subsequent sets of horses were the fastest long-distance runners available. Using the relay system, the outlaws could keep up a consistent rapid pace across even daunting desert terrain, while the posse in pursuit ran out of steam early on. The lawmen often had to rest their horses overnight—or longer—while Butch and his men continued without stopping, putting hundreds of miles between them and the law.

With so many myths surrounding Butch and the Wild Bunch, it can be difficult to separate fact from fiction. It can be just as difficult to determine exactly which robberies—of banks, trains, payrolls, and mines—were Butch's doing. Sometimes his signature was unmistakable, but there were likely other jobs for which he was not credited.

While Butch consistently flirted with the law and pulled off an unknown number of small heists in the intervening years, the first robbery known to be committed by the Wild Bunch after they were organized was that of a bank in Montpelier, Idaho. It had been seven years since Butch had robbed a bank.

The scrupulous planning for which Butch was famous went into the robbery from the beginning. A series of secret meetings were conducted in the weeks before the heist, and Butch spent time rounding up teams of relay horses. He chose two of his most trusted gang members— Elza Lay and Bub Meeks—to help him, and the three of them landed honest employment on a ranch north of town, where they continued to make plans and keep an eye on the lay of the land.

Two days before the planned robbery, the trio quit their jobs at the ranch and headed for Monpelier. They settled around a table at a nearby saloon on the afternoon of August 13, 1896, and waited for the bank to close.

Just before the bank closed, as was his habit, the cashier emerged from the bank and started talking to a friend on the sidewalk. What happened next moved with rapid precision. Butch and Elza, guns concealed, ordered the cashier and his friend back into the bank; Elza held up the cashier, a teller, and a female stenographer, forcing them against the wall while Butch gathered up more than $7,100—the equivalent of $136,000 today—in cash, gold, and silver. Meeks, sporting a Stetson banded with rattlesnake rattles, waited outside the bank with the getaway horses.

Though a posse was immediately organized and took off in hot pursuit of the bandits, it was no match for Butch's carefully arranged relay teams. After trying to catch the three outlaws for almost a week, the posse gave up and returned in defeat to Montpelier. Legend has it that the outlaws fled east to the Wind River and then south to Rock Springs, where they spent part of their loot on a defense attorney for Matt Warner, who had been accused of murder in a separate incident.

Just eight months later the gang executed their only major robbery in Utah and one of their most spectacular ever. The Pleasant Valley Coal Company had set up coal mining operations in Castle Gate, just outside Price, and had quickly become somewhat tyrannical. The company not only owned all the land in Castle Gate, but every building as well. The miners who underwent backbreaking labor were little more than slaves: Those who wanted to keep their jobs—critical in the sparse circumstances of the Wild West—had to rent their homes from the company and buy every necessity from the company store.

No one could have predicted what was about to happen on Wednesday, April 21, 1897. Butch sat on a chair against the wall outside the payroll office, his hat pulled low and looking for all the world like he was taking a nap. Elza lounged casually on his own horse nearby, holding another horse as if merely waiting for a friend to finish his business in one of the establishments along the sidewalk.

As the Rio Grande Western passenger train ground to a halt outside the coal mine offices, the Pleasant Valley Coal Company paymaster and two armed guards emerged from the train with a bag of cash— the company's entire $8,000 payroll (more than $150,000 today). He meandered past Butch without even glancing in his direction—until, that is, Butch lunged forward, stuck a gun in the paymaster's ribs, yanked the bag away from him, and tossed it to Elza before leaping onto his own horse. Mounted on the fastest race horses they could find, Butch and Elza disappeared down the road toward Price. The armed men who guarded the paymaster stood helplessly by, never even attempting to stop the two outlaws. (Some theorize that's because the company was widely detested and was finally the victim.)

In Price, Butch and Elza mounted long-distance runners who could maintain a rapid gallop over miles of open desert. They figured they had gotten easily away, especially since the telegraph wires had been cut, but didn't count on the factor of two different posses—one bringing up the rear, the other speeding toward Price by locomotive, the same train that had delivered the payroll. The posses eventually organized in nearby Castle Dale and Price galloped at full speed toward Buckhorn Wash, where they intended to cut off the outlaws' escape.

Sure enough, the first posse to reach Buckhorn Wash set up an ambush. When they saw riders approaching, they opened fire—then quickly realized they were firing not on the outlaws but on the other posse. The outlaws had somehow eluded the law and slipped into Robbers' Roost. They were never apprehended.

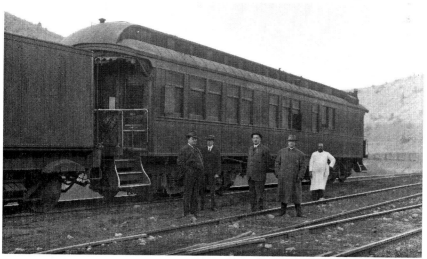

Train at Castle Gate, Utah, where Butch Cassidy and his gang robbed the Pleasant Valley Coal Company payroll, their only major robbery in the state of Utah.

Buckhorn Wash, the site of a shootout between two posses, each of which thought they were shooting at outlaws.

The jobs got increasingly bigger and more lucrative. On June 2, 1899, the Wild Bunch held up the Overland Flyer train near Wilcox, Wyoming, getting away with more than $60,000—almost $1.2 million in today's currency. Besides escaping, none of the Wild Bunch was injured in the subsequent shootout.

Encouraged by the success of the Overland Flyer job, the gang pulled off its next train robbery just a month later on July 11, 1899. They escaped with their biggest payoff ever, getting an unprecedented $70,000 (equivalent to $1.33 million today) from a Rio Grande train near Folsom, New Mexico. Butch masterminded the heist, though he was not directly involved in it.

Lawmen were determined to help the railroad recover the stolen loot and pursued the gang in earnest. A few days after the heist, lawmen did catch up with the outlaws; in the subsequent shootout, Elza Lay shot and killed a sheriff. Captured and convicted, he was sentenced to life in prison. It was the second "right-hand man" Butch had lost to a prison sentence.

According to theory, Elza's arrest and imprisonment started gnawing at Butch, and he decided to abandon his outlaw life if he could obtain clemency for the string of train robberies he had committed. Butch wrote to both Utah Governor Heber Wells and the Union Pacific Railroad—the target of many of his holdups—to see if they'd agree to a bold arrangement: Butch would stop holding up Union Pacific trains if the company would agree not to prosecute Butch for any of the train robberies that had occurred.

A meeting was arranged between Butch and Union Pacific officials. Butch arrived as promised. Unfortunately—and unbeknownst to Butch—the railroad officials were held up by a storm and arrived at the agreed-upon rendezvous spot a day late. Butch was gone, and in his place was a hastily scrawled note. All deals were off.

Railroad officials were in a panic, as was the governor. They desperately wanted to bring an end to the dramatic (and lucrative) train robberies, so they hatched their own plan. They recruited former outlaw and Butch's initial right-hand man, Matt Warner—who had just been released from jail and who had abandoned his outlaw ways—to track down Butch, explain the Union Pacific delay, and plead for compliance with the original terms of the proposal. They again agreed not to prosecute if Butch would stop robbing trains.

It was a short-lived prospect. On his way to find Butch, Matt Warner received a telegram. Never mind, it said—Butch had just robbed another train, this one near Tipton, Wyoming. Butch and four of his Wild Bunch were recognized and identified by passengers on the train, and the take was more than $55,000.

According to eyewitnesses, a single masked bandit boarded the train waving his pistol, and told the engineer to stop when he saw a campfire near the tracks. The terrified engineer complied. After the train pulled to a stop, four more desperadoes clamored on board, using dynamite to blast the doors off the safes. It held the trademark of a Butch Cassidy job: Seeing the terror on the crew members' faces, one

After having moved from cattle rustling to bank robbing, Butch Cassidy spent the last part of his outlaw career robbing trains—a crime that led to a far higher payoff with less risk.

of the outlaws promised that no one would get hurt. He even went so far as to vow that he would murder one of his own men if anyone on board the train was accidentally killed.

Railroad officials reneged on their offer of clemency. They were fiercely determined to pursue the outlaws and prosecute them to the fullest extent of the law. Their prize would be the kingpin himself, Butch Cassidy.

They failed. As for Butch, he narrowly evaded capture. Not sure how much longer his luck would hold out against the enraged railroad officials who were renewing efforts to capture him, he decided it was time to prepare to leave the country. He began working with his accomplice from the Tipton job—longtime partner Harry Longabaugh, "the Sundance Kid"—to make arrangements for a permanent getaway.

Formulating a plan to flee to South America, where he would be safe from the law in the United States, Butch organized his gang for two more bank robberies to finance his plan. On September 9, 1900, the outlaws got away with $32,640—a little more than $620,000 in to-day's currency—from a bank in Winnemucca, Nevada. The final heist credited to Butch Cassidy and the Wild Bunch was another train rob-bery, particularly daring considering he was solidly in the crosshairs of the railroad officials. This time they got away with $65,000—equivalent to more than $1.2 million today—on July 3, 1901, from the Northern Pacific train near Wagner, Montana.

It was time for the Wild Bunch to scatter. Their familiar territory had become more populated, making it increasingly more difficult to avoid capture. The law enforcement agencies they had repeatedly evaded started successfully anticipating their antics, becoming much better organized. And the railroads, weary of being such lucrative targets for the outlaws, hired the Pinkerton's National Detective Agency to hunt down and capture Butch. For the first time, he had a serious target painted on his back.

Feeling his days were numbered, Butch took longtime partner Harry Longabaugh and Etta Place—a member of the Wild Bunch with whom both men had been romantically involved—to South America, where they bought a ranch in Argentina. After a few years of trying to make an honest living, they resorted to the easiest way they knew to raise cash: robbing banks and trains.

Harry Longabaugh (the Sundance Kid) and Etta Place.

Historians know of a few successful robberies they committed in South America, but from there the trail grows . . . well, if not cold, then at least mysterious. Those who saw the movie might go with the theory that Butch Cassidy and the Sundance Kid were gunned down by Bolivian officials in 1908 in a dramatic scene worthy of Hollywood. But that may not be the truth; no one knows, exactly.

Some say the pair let officials believe they had been killed in Bolivia while they quietly returned to America's West, where they lived out their lives under various aliases. Butch's sister, Lula Betenson, steadfastly claimed he was present at a family gathering in Utah in 1925, where he had the chance to make peace with his father.[48] Another account says he died of stomach cancer in 1937. Still other accounts place his death as late as 1941.[49]

The truth? *You* decide.

CHAPTER FOUR
Matt Warner, "The Mormon Kid"

JUST ABOUT ANY WAY YOU cut it, Matt Warner wasn't your typical outlaw. He went from a law-abiding, religious existence to life as an outlaw—and then back again, spending his final days as a deputy sheriff, night guard, and justice of the peace. Even during his action-packed bank-robbing days, he rarely used his gun—and then only in self-defense. Unlike many outlaws who embraced violence, Matt prided himself on his gentlemanly conduct, whether rustling cattle or robbing a bank.

A handful of other things set Matt Warner apart too. For one, he was a family man, rare among the outlaws of the Old West; his first wife died while he was in prison, and he married a second upon his release. He had children to whom he was devoted. He wrote a memoir—and while some believe he exaggerated the facts at times, he's one of very few outlaws known to have put an autobiographical pen to paper. And he died a peaceful death of natural causes at

Matt Warner near Price, Utah, in 1937. Following decades of outlaw behavior, Matt became a lawman.

an old age while almost all of his outlaw colleagues died in shootouts with the law or fellow bandits.

But perhaps the oddest thing that sets Matt Warner apart is that his foray into a life of crime was the result of a tragic misunderstanding—the fallout from a romantic rivalry that reared its ugly head when he was only fourteen.

Matt Warner was born Willard Erastus Christianson in 1864 in Ephraim, Utah, the son of a Swedish father and a German mother—devoted Mormon converts who had immigrated to Utah as part of the influx of pioneers. As a young child, he and his family witnessed the Ephraim Indian Massacre, an attack in which the Ute leader Black Hawk raided a cattle ranch and took out any who tried to interfere. By the time it was over, five settlers, including two women, lay dead. The Christianson family fled north to Levan, where Matt's father began farming and opened a small store.

Matt's life of crime almost got an even earlier start than it did due to another simple misunderstanding. Arriving at the store one afternoon, Matt—still known as Willard at the time—found a Ute brave engaged in animated conversation with his father. Assuming the Indian was trying to rob his father, young Matt pulled out a pistol in a misguided act of bravado—an attempt to protect his father from what

Main Street in Ephraim, where Willard Erastus Christianson (Matt Warner) spent his childhood.

he perceived was a genuine threat. (After all, this was a child who had witnessed an Indian massacre not many years before.) Just as he was about to pull the trigger, his father set him straight.

Matt never cared much for farming, but he loved horses. As a young teenager, he was so good with them that he was hired to break wild mustangs, exciting work that he relished. By the time he was fourteen, he landed a job as a cowboy and was tasked with helping drive a herd to Wyoming—action-packed work for a kid eager to leave the farm. But he only got as far as Roosevelt, a few hundred miles, when he was overcome by lovesickness for a pretty girl back home. Matt left his job as a cowboy, pointed his trusty steed in the direction of home, and galloped as quickly as he could back to Levan and pretty little Alice Sabey. The return trip, smack through the middle of Indian territory, held plenty of adventure itself.

As it turned out, pretty little Alice Sabey played a major but completely unintentional role in launching fourteen-year-old Willard Erastus Christianson into life as an outlaw. Willard made it safely through Indian territory and promptly began courting Alice as soon as he arrived, breathless, in Levan. Things were going pretty well until, as they do, things got complicated. As it turns out, someone else also had his eye on Alice. And that someone else—a bully named Andrew Hendricksen—wasn't about to let Willard be the only contender for Alice's heart.

One Saturday night after a church dance, Willard and Andrew were both walking Alice home when Andrew started pushing Willard around. Willard didn't like it. Andrew got increasingly more aggressive. There was a strict code of conduct in small Mormon towns, and part of it dictated that you *never* fought in front of a lady. Well, Andrew violated that code. During a brief moment while Alice was distracted, Andrew punched Willard, then sealed the deal by reaching over and tweaking his nose. Alice flew into a panic. She favored Willard but didn't know how to handle the attention from Andrew. Frightened that a full-fledged fight was about to erupt between the two, she bolted through her gate and ran into her house.

Once Alice was safely out of the picture, a full-fledged fight *did* erupt. Normally quiet, soft-spoken, and gentle, Willard could have a real temper when pushed—and he felt pushed. A veritable brawl broke out, attracting the attention of both boys' friends, who stood on the sidelines and egged them on.

In a moment of wild anger, Willard did something that would change the course of his life: he picked up a good-sized rock and whacked his rival squarely on the head. Andrew's eyes rolled back into his head and he slumped to the ground. Still seething with rage, Willard broke off a piece of Alice's fence and proceeded to beat the bully to a pulp.[50] Reflecting on the incident in his memoir, Willard wrote, "I always will believe that my life might have been different if it hadn't been for something that happened to me one summer night when I was between fourteen and fifteen years old."[51]

As his temper calmed, he heard the panic-stricken voices of the boys on the sidelines crying that Andrew was dead. Andrew's brother Moroni started screaming for someone to find the marshal. Willard focused in on his victim with more than a little panic himself. For all intents and purposes, Andrew *did* look dead. Convinced he had committed murder, Willard dropped the piece of wooden fence he had used as a weapon and sprinted for home, where he quickly packed his bags, confessed his misdeed to his parents, bid them an anguished farewell, and rode north as fast as he could.

His thoughts kept rhythm with the horse's pounding hooves. He was only fourteen—still a boy, really—but he figured he could be arrested and hanged for murder. Who knew? They might already be pursuing him. He was sure there was a bounty on his head. He would never see the beautiful Alice Sabey again, but that was a small price to pay for his freedom and his life.

The next morning, exhausted, he stopped at a freighter near Indianola, where he hoped to get some breakfast. When the man who pushed a tin plate of scrambled eggs toward Willard asked his name, Willard realized for the first time that he could no longer use his real name. He was wanted, a fugitive on the run. So he said the first thing that came into his mind: "I'm Matt Warner." The name stuck. (It stuck so solidly, in fact, that after he left his life of crime and became a law-abiding citizen again, he had his name legally changed to Matt Warner.)

Meanwhile, back at the ranch, Andrew Hendricksen was anything *but* dead. Hearing the uproar in front of the house, Alice's parents rushed out as Willard was running from the scene. They administered aid to the injured boy, nursed his wounds, and helped him get back home. He recovered. He even initially had an apparent change of heart, telling anyone who would listen that he had behaved badly and deserved the beating Willard dished out. (And who knows? Maybe he eventually captured the heart of pretty little Alice Sabey.)

As it turns out, Andrew wasn't dead, but folks claim he was never "really the same" again. Some say it was the beating that rattled his brains. Others say it was his long-term exposure to mercury and lead, courtesy of the potter he worked with for years. Whatever the cause, Andrew did something very unexpected one balmy summer day. As the city of Levan prepared to start its annual parade—just about the biggest event each year—the parade marshal, a respected and highly revered citizen of Levan, sat atop his steed smoothing his shirt, adjusting his spurs, and making sure his hat was sitting just right. Out of the blue, Andrew Henricksen rode up, put a pistol in the parade marshal's face, and blew him clean off his horse—in front of dozens of witnesses. Andrew made a quick getaway and spent a few days hiding in a barn, but the law eventually found him and arrested him for the murder. No one, including Andrew, could figure out exactly what provoked him. He spent the rest of his days in an insane asylum with a world of space between him and his gun. But we digress.

Willard didn't know that Andrew survived, or that he initially felt he had a beating coming to him, or that Andrew himself was the killer. No, Willard Erastus Christianson figured he himself was beyond redemption. He believed he had committed murder. It was a mistaken belief that informed his behavior for the next two or three decades. Simply put, he embraced an outlaw lifestyle over a murder that never happened.

Years later, when he realized that Andrew Hendricksen was alive and well, Matt wrote that life "shoved me out on the bandit trail for a murder never committed and that didn't happen. When I found out I wasn't a murderer, it was too late; life had already made an outlaw out of me."[52] Matt typified what former President Theodore Roosevelt described when he wrote, "Often [outlaws] are people who in certain stages of civilization do, or have done, good work, but who, when these

Matt Warner, left, with an unknown outlaw.

stages have passed, find themselves surrounded by conditions which accentuate their worst qualities and make their best qualities useless."[53]

Seized with terror over what he believed had happened that Saturday night after the church dance, Matt rode as fast as he could back through Indian territory, praying all the while that he could reach safety and somehow regain his job as a cowboy. But try though he did, he never succeeded in tracking down the herd he had deserted. The other cowhands had driven it too quickly out of range. Now only fifteen, Matt found himself on Diamond Mountain outside Vernal—a peak named for a diamond scam years earlier and located on the fringes of Brown's Hole, the famous outlaw hideaway. As far as being schooled in outlawry, Matt could not have happened on a better campus.

Matt liked Diamond Mountain, a rugged section of land peppered with cowboys and outlaws, and he especially liked the fact that no one there knew about his alleged murderous past. Displaying his impressive cowboy skills, he was able to land a job with Diamond Mountain rancher Jim Warren, who eagerly took Matt under his wing and taught him a passel of ranching skills.

That wasn't the only thing he taught young Matt. In those days, even the legitimate ranchers almost always combined ranching with a little cattle rustling to beef up their income. Warren was only too happy to tutor Matt in those skills as well, and Matt became stunningly proficient with a branding iron. He got paid a man's wage for doing a man's work, despite his tender age, and got along well with the other ranch hands Warren employed. Though he was beginning to abandon the strict religious practices of his faith, the other employees on the ranch affectionately called him "the Mormon Kid," a nickname that followed him throughout his outlaw days.

With Warren's help and a good dose of his own hard work, Matt soon had enough cattle for a herd of his own and the means to build his own home and ranch. By the time he reached the tender age of twenty, he was a part-time rancher, part-time outlaw who was well-acquainted with both whisky and poker. While Andrew Hendricksen was pursuing life back in Levan and regions round about, being exposed to all that mercury and lead, Matt had become, for all intents and purposes, a gentlemanly outlaw.

He had also become a legendary gunman, fiercely accurate with both a Winchester and a Colt. He owed most of it to practice: he would tie a beer bottle to a tree branch with a length of string, send the bottle spinning, run a few steps in the opposite direction, then turn and shoot. He never missed—not even up against a wildly gyrating beer bottle. He once told a lawman he had spent more than a year's wages on bullets, "because I know someday I'll have to shoot my way out."

All that practice came in handy one afternoon when Matt ended up in a quick-draw duel with a Mexican gunslinger named Polito who had stolen Matt's horse. Duels were a common way of settling disputes in those days, and Matt agreed to the duel in an attempt to recover his property. He was lucky: Polito was faster on the draw, but Matt was more accurate, sending a bullet into his opponent's lung. Most outlaws would have called it over, but what happened next was a typical show of Matt Warner's basic character. Rushing to Polito's side, he administered aid and made sure he was stable, then rode twenty miles to fetch a doctor. He continued to nurse Polito at his own ranch until the man fully recovered.

Matt's ranch was flourishing but didn't provide enough of a thrill for the young man whose occasional criminal activities had done little more than whet his appetite. He had watched from afar as his brother-in-law, Tom McCarty, had built a thriving business as an outlaw.

Outlawry was literally happening all around him, often at the hand of legitimate ranchers and storekeepers. Matt's regular association with the outlaws who inhabited Brown's Hole eventually left him wanting more excitement, and that excitement initially came in the form of outlaw Elza Lay, who was cooking up the details of what he considered to be a perfect crime.

Elza—real name, William Ellsworth Lay—was a well-educated cowboy who always had at least one book in his saddlebag and who was well-known for his intellectual curiosity. Migrating through the Utah Territory from Texas with a herd of cattle, he loved the Rocky Mountains and decided to stay, eventually moving to Brown's Hole and taking up with the outlaws who tipped him into their lifestyle. Finding it difficult to live the good life on a cowhand's wages, he had started dabbling in outlaw activities to supplement his income, though he often served only as the brains behind the criminal schemes that he persuaded others to carry out. Some, in fact, believe he was the brains behind many of Butch Cassidy's antics.

Enter Matt Warner. This one was a cinch, Elza explained. A Jewish storeowner in Wyoming had gone out of business, largely because he was so unpopular. His creditors were planning to confiscate his merchandise and sell it at auction in the attempt to settle his debts with them. But Elza figured out a way to take advantage of the situation: He'd send Matt and Matt's nephew to the store in the dark of night, have them steal all the merchandise, then sell it in Vernal—and split the profits, of course. And here was the real joke of it all: the storeowner was in on the plot and stood to get a piece of the action. As a result of that genius part of the plan, the outlaws were guaranteed protection from the storeowner. After all, he had participated in literally stealing the merchandise from his creditors too. No way would he cooperate with officials trying to solve the crime.

It worked. It was relatively carefree, law enforcement stayed out of it, nobody died, and everybody in on the deal got a handsome profit. It was just the adrenalin blast a bored Matt needed to spice things up. He was hooked.

From then on, Matt started straying further and further into criminal activity. He spent increasingly longer periods of time away from his ranch, often leaving it in the capable hands of good friends—

Matt Warner's name inscribed on a rock at Buckhorn Wash, near Robbers' Roost.

including Moroni Hendricksen, the brother of Matt's supposed murder victim whose cries for the marshal had sent Matt running all those years earlier. As much as he loved his ranch and horses, he would grow restless after a week or two at home and would do whatever possible to find a new adventure.

During these and other exploits, Matt became known for his courteous behavior and gentlemanly ways. As mentioned, he never liked to use his gun against another soul. In his memoirs, he opined that for outlaws, killing "becomes an appetite and has to be fed like hunger or thirst."[54] Shying away from any association with outlaws who were killers,[55] he wrote that he shot only out of self-defense—and one time he discharged his pistol just "to scare" another man, "not to kill him."[56]

He even became known as a sort of Robin Hood to the residents of Brown's Hole, sometimes stealing from the rich and giving most of the proceeds to the poor. He built a tremendous network of friends who were often the recipients of his generosity. Explaining one such escapade in his memoirs, he wrote, "Suddenly their poverty wrung our hearts. We was [sic] convinced the only right and manly thing to do was give these goods to the poor and lowly of Brown's Park."[57]

Matt soon discovered that his legitimate earnings from ranching and his ill-gotten gains from random rustling escapades simply didn't pay the bills or provide him with the kind of lifestyle for which he yearned. With some trepidation, he decided to move on to more lucrative work.

And so Matt decided to try his hand at robbery. He and a two-bit outlaw named Joe, an acquaintance from Brown's Hole, held up a bank and its attached general store in St. Johns, Arizona, making off with $897—the equivalent of more than $17,000 in today's dollars. When the local sheriff unexpectedly gave chase with a posse of trained officers, the two ditched into Robbers' Roost to evade arrest. It was the closest Matt had come to actually being nabbed by the law, and he was nervous. All the emotions he felt on his panic-stricken escape from Levan came rushing back, bringing all kinds of regret and fear.

The *last* thing Matt wanted was to be arrested, so the pair stayed holed up in the Roost for several months until they felt safe traveling on the outside again. Joe headed north, beating a path back to Diamond Mountain. Matt—realizing that, whether he liked it or not, the bank robbery had made of him a real outlaw—went in search of help in the form of his brother-in-law Tom McCarty, a seasoned outlaw who had married his older sister. He reckoned Tom could help him figure out what to do next—and could likely help him stay a few paces ahead of the law.

He finally met up with Tom and another outlaw in Fort Wingate, Arizona. Matt had arrived just in time to form a partnership with the other two on a cattle raid in Mexico. Still squeamish from his near-capture a few months earlier, Matt expressed hesitation, but Tom assured him it was a safe deal. Screwing up all his courage, Matt finally agreed to help in the heist. Sure enough, it went off without a hitch. The trio safely brought two hundred cattle back into New Mexico, where they sold them for $3.50 a head—a tidy profit of more than $13,000 in today's dollars. It was just the kind of job that convinced Matt that maybe crime *did* pay after all.

The first one went so well that Tom and Matt rounded up another accomplice and planned a second cattle raid in Mexico. The raid itself went smooth as glass, but when they crossed the border into United States territory, armed federal marshals hunted them in hot pursuit, almost apprehending them numerous times. The resulting chase took them over six hundred miles of the roughest terrain in the area;

they finally managed to permanently lose the officers just outside the Robbers' Roost area.

Their accomplice, who was badly wounded by the marshals, miraculously survived the trip. Matt and Tom dropped him off with friends in Kanab who agreed to nurse him back to health. Matt and Tom kept going, heading north to Frisco, a mining camp west of Milford.

The Horn Silver Mine—which would produce $20 million worth of silver over the next decade—had recently been discovered. Eventually extending more than nine hundred feet into the ground and supported by timbers, it was one of the first open-pit mines in the west. But it wasn't just the silver that brought miners from all over the west to Frisco: gold, copper, lead, and zinc were also extracted from the numerous mines in the area.

Minerals may have been plentiful, but drinking water had to be freighted in to Frisco. But such an inconvenience didn't keep the rough-and-tumble element in town at bay. Boasting twenty-three saloons, Frisco was the wildest town in the Utah Territory; murders were frequent, and no one ever knew exactly how long they could hold on to their pay.

Street scene in Frisco, a rough-and-tumble mining settlement west of Millard and home of the Horn Silver Mine, where many outlaws frequented the settlement's twenty-three saloons.

Coke ovens at the site of Frisco, a mining camp that yielded silver, gold, copper, lead, and zinc. Saloons at the camp were frequented by the Mormon outlaws.

The perilously constructed open-pit mine suddenly collapsed on February 13, 1885, bringing Frisco's silver glory days to a screeching halt. But Frisco was still at its peak when Matt and Tom arrived. Wanting to capitalize on such a perfect market for beef, the pair bought—not rustled—a small herd of cattle and drove it to Frisco, ready to cash in handsomely. But things didn't work as they had intended. Town marshal Billy Sackett, familiar with their exploits in New Mexico, arrested them for rustling and took them to Milford to stand trial.

Marshal Sackett was filled with righteous indignation about the rustling that had gone on in New Mexico, and he wanted to keep any more unsavory elements out of Frisco. But the judge in Milford was hard-pressed to figure out how to make the charges stick when Matt and Tom had legally purchased the cattle they brought into Frisco. With no other option in his mind, he acquitted the pair. Sackett was furious, and he was convinced that even if they hadn't rustled the cattle they brought into town, the two had committed crimes there that he just didn't know about. In retaliation for their acquittal, he made the two walk the fifteen miles back to Frisco.

A bad taste in their mouths for the mining camp, Matt and Tom decided to put Frisco behind them. Within minutes of arriving at the destination of their long, dusty walk, they mounted their horses and rode about forty miles west to the "ranch" of Tom "Black Jack" Ketchum, a known hideout for outlaws. It was their intention to cool their heels, recover from their mistreatment in Frisco, and take a break away from the prying eyes of the law.

That's not quite what happened, though. Never underestimate the wrath of a marshal spurned. Within a few short days, two men—undoubtedly dispatched by Sackett—arrived at the ranch, claiming to be prospectors in search of a mining opportunity. Something didn't seem quite right to Tom, who held tight to his pistol while he examined the men and their rucksacks. Sure enough, he discovered two pairs of handcuffs, obviously intended for him and Matt. Slapping the handcuffs on the officers, he confiscated their rucksacks and sent them off into the unforgiving desert, cuffed and on foot. Facing a forty-mile walk to Frisco, things looked pretty hopeless for the officers.

Their initial despair only deepened when they heard the beating hooves of Tom's horse. Obviously, he had decided to kill them rather than make them face the desolate march across the desert. But they didn't know Tom and Matt, men who still clung to some vestiges of their religious upbringing. Persuaded by Matt, Tom had relented. He released the cuffs, freed the officers, gave them each a canteen filled with water, and wished them good luck. Then, bidding them good-bye, he rode back to Ketchum's hideout.

Matt was exhausted by all the uproar. When Tom decided to go to Cortez, Colorado, in search of other exploits, Matt decided to call it a day and head back to his ranch at Diamond Mountain. When he arrived, he didn't get the kind of reception he was hoping for: Instead of a desperately needed chance to relax, he found he was still a subject of great interest to the law, who sought his arrest on rustling charges. Feeling he had no other option, he gathered the horses he owned and drove them to an area near Meeker, Colorado, in the verdant White River country.

But even there Matt couldn't relax. When he sold a hundred horses to a man in Meeker, Matt was paid in hundred-dollar bills—a bankroll that attracted a lot of attention when he checked into a local boardinghouse. By now suspicious, maybe even a little paranoid, Matt kept a careful eye on everyone around him. The next day, two men from the boardinghouse who had seen Matt's cash approached on horseback, intending to hold him up. But Matt recognized them and was ready, gun drawn; he held *them* up instead. Recognizing that he wasn't in friendly territory, he retreated to the La Sal Mountains in southeastern Utah, where the McCarty family had owned a ranch.

Arriving at the ranch, Matt discovered that Tom's father and brother had moved to Oregon years earlier. Tom and his other brother, Bill, had sold the ranch, gambled away the money, and become full-time outlaws. Wanting to take a break from a life of crime, Matt—now twenty-one—established himself in the area and started training horses to race.

That year Matt's life again took a dramatic turn. At a horse race in Telluride, Colorado, he met a nineteen-year-old ore hauler with whom he had several pivotal things in common. First of all, they both loved horses, and the younger man displayed just as much aptitude at training them. Second, they had both grown up in the Mormon Church but strayed off the beaten path. They hit it off famously—and Matt Warner and Butch Cassidy agreed to become partners in a horse-racing business operating out of Utah, Colorado, Wyoming, and New Mexico.

Using a horse named Betty (Bebe in some accounts), they won every race they entered. After running a hard but successful race in southern Colorado, Matt went to Cortez to look up his brother-in-law and former partner in crime, Tom McCarty. It was the first time Tom McCarty and Butch Cassidy met. They became great friends, and Tom joined them in their horse-racing escapades.

They became absolutely revered on the horse-racing circuit, and soon no one other than Indians would agree to race them. In one memorable race, Betty performed admirably, and they won not only an Indian's pony but a load of blankets as well. Tom didn't have nearly the finesse Matt did and had a bit of a hair-trigger temper. When the Indian objected to the earnings, Tom beat him with a braided leather whip before Matt and Tom fled to Tom's cabin.

That wasn't the end of it, though. The next morning the Indians arrived at the cabin, demanding the horse back. Discussions were heated but fairly innocent until one of the Indians pointed his rifle at Tom. Always a quick draw, Tom shot the Indian off his horse—and the others beat a hasty retreat.

For two years until late 1887, the three were content to race horses and occasionally work as ranch hands. While the activity was legal, their earnings tended to slip through their fingers far too quickly, spent on fast-paced poker games and gallons of whisky. In order to cover their daily expenses, they were forced to turn to rustling and other outlaw activities. Before long, they were known as the McCarty Gang.

A number of high-profile jobs during the next few years were credited to the McCarty Gang—and specifically Matt Warner—even though the evidence was never strong enough to indict them. On November 3, 1887, the Denver & Rio Grande train was held up just outside Grand Junction, Colorado; the holdup men—believed to be Butch Cassidy, Tom McCarty, and Matt Warner—blocked the track and acted with efficiency but didn't make off with any cash.

The next caper credited to Matt was much more lucrative. On March 30, 1889, a man walked into the First National Bank of Denver and asked to see the bank president. Producing a bottle of liquid that he claimed to be an explosive, he demanded $21,000—almost $400,000 in today's currency. In fear of his life, the president produced the cash. The bandit coolly walked out of the bank, handed the money to an accomplice, and vanished into the crowd. All evidence pointed to Matt Warner as the accomplice.

Just a few months later the McCarty Gang, accompanied by Butch Cassidy's younger brother and a fifth accomplice, robbed the San Miguel Valley Bank in Telluride, Colorado, and easily got away with an unprecedented amount of cash from a slower posse of law enforcement officers. The only casualty from the job came when Butch's younger brother got arrested on old charges while transporting supplies to the outlaws and lost his share of the take.

That winter Matt and Tom had plenty of money to sustain themselves, and they took some time off in picturesque Star Valley, Wyoming, nestled along the Utah border just south of Jackson, where they used the aliases Matt Willard and Tom Smith. While there, Matt married fourteen-year-old Rosa Rumel. By now widowed, Tom married a woman named Sarah Lemberg. Butch Cassidy went his separate way.

It was a harsh winter, and times were tough in Star Valley. When the only storekeeper in Afton, Wyoming, refused to extend credit to the desperate settlers, Matt's Robin Hood mentality kicked in. He and Tom held the storekeeper at gunpoint while the settlers took what they needed from the store. When the last settler had cleared out, Matt

The merchantile in Green River where Matt Warner and other outlaws purchased supplies for Robbers' Roost; those staying there tried to appoint it with the comforts of home.

paid the storekeeper half the going price for the goods that had been taken—using, of course, part of his proceeds from the Telluride job.

When the spring thaw arrived, Matt and Tom took their wives and settled in Butte, Montana, where they managed to spend the rest of their proceeds from Telluride. With the last of their money, they sent their wives back to Star Valley while they went to Haines, Oregon, to reunite with the rest of Tom's family. Sadly, the family had fallen on hard times, and it took little effort to convince Tom's brother Bill to be a third partner in a series of small robberies. (After Telluride, *everything* seemed small.)

The first of the robberies resulted in only enough money for Matt to send for Rosa. Despite initial misgivings, she came. For her part, Sarah refused to come.

The family moved to Cooley, Washington, when lawmen in Haines started suspecting their involvement in local robberies. There, they bought the 7-U Ranch, a headquarters from which they ran a series of robberies in Washington and Oregon that kept them supplied with operating capital.

Rosa, weary of the outlaw life and sick of the constant moves, begged Matt to settle down and abandon his outlaw ways. Her sister,

Sadie Morgan, had come to live with them and also harassed Matt to get clean and settle down in an area where her sister could live in peace. Rosa was expecting a baby, and she feared for the child's future if her husband continued as an outlaw.

Rosa's pleas fell on sympathetic ears. Just a few days before his daughter was born, Matt and the others robbed $20,000—almost $400,000 in today's currency—from a bank in Roslyn, Washington. They were almost captured in a furious chase but managed to elude officials. When he got home, he made a solemn promise to Rosa: Within the next few days, he said, he would take his share of the funds, dig up the rest of his stash, and leave the gang. He and Rosa, he promised, would make a fresh start, and he would find a legitimate way to support their family.

Almost as soon as the promise rolled off his tongue, Matt was arrested. The next day, Tom's father, George McCarty, was arrested as well and put in Matt's cell. The lawyer who arrived to defend Matt told him he

could be freed if he could put enough money in the right hands. Matt drew a map to the exact spot where his stash was buried—all $41,000 of it (just shy of $800,000 to us)—and told the lawyer to take what he needed.

Even though they unsuccessfully tried to escape—hardly the model prisoners—the pair was soon freed. A shocked Matt learned, much to his dismay, that his freedom had cost his entire fortune: $41,000. In a "goodwill"

Matt Warner, top right, in 1902, two years after he reformed, with two former gunmen and a lawyer.

gesture (more likely to avoid all kinds of potential problems from an infuriated outlaw), the lawyer gave Matt $500 of "his own" money.

An estimate of Matt's take from his three-year bank robbery career totals about $1.35 million in today's currency—plenty to sustain even a high-roller for life. But Matt had managed to lose it all. Broke and down on his luck, Matt found the 7-U Ranch completely vandalized and destroyed by bounty hunters. Trading the ranch for a strong horse and a good saddle, Matt went back to Diamond Mountain. Despite the fact that Rosa's sister and mother had accused Matt of abusing Rosa, charges he vehemently denied throughout the rest of his life, Rosa joined him at Diamond Mountain, and the two lived a quiet, peaceful existence there for two years.

Sadly, Rosa developed bone cancer in her leg, and she and Matt spent much of the next few years in Vernal, where she received treatment. Matt had made good his promise and had avoided any further outlaw activities, undoubtedly aided by the fact that most of Tom's family had been killed after robbing another bank, something in which Matt was not involved. After a shootout at the bank, Tom left the area permanently.

Even though Matt stayed away from the outlaws, yet another misunderstanding would again change the course of his life. When a friend of his became convinced that a trio of men was trying to steal his mining claim, he hired Matt and local gambler Bill Wall to merely frighten the men off. That remained their intent, but things went bad, as they often do.

When tempers flared and the situation escalated, a sudden gun battle erupted. The three outlaws were no match for Matt and Bill. When the smoke cleared, two were dead—shot in self-defense. The third was severely wounded, crippled for life.

Despite compelling evidence that Matt and Bill had acted in self-defense, prosecutors saw their opportunity to punish Matt for a whole string of past crimes. Even though his friends intervened (and used their proceeds from a bank robbery in Montpelier, Idaho, to pay his defense attorney), Matt was found guilty of murder and was sent to the Utah State Penitentiary on September 21, 1896.

Rosa was devastated, as was Matt. While he was in prison, Rosa gave birth to a son, Rex (who would not survive past his childhood), and shortly thereafter she died of the bone cancer that had afflicted her. In a show of mercy, officials allowed Matt to leave prison—heavily guarded, of course—to attend her funeral.

Describing his feelings at her death, Matt wrote, "I guess a man never went through more agony and lived than I did when they took me handcuffed between two guards to see my dead wife lying there in the coffin and that weak, puny, shriveled, half-dead baby in the arms of its accusing grandmother. That was all my past, all my responsibility rising up all together and handing me a knockout right on the chin."[58] Realizing that his infant son, who was adopted by a Salina couple, would never know him as his father, Matt agonized, "This is the price I had to pay for my outlaw life. It is the biggest price a man can pay for anything."[59]

Humbled with regret for his past misdeeds and the resulting impact on his life, Matt was the model prisoner. Utah Governor Heber M. Wells became captivated by Matt and granted a pardon. Released early because of the pardon and for good behavior, he left prison on January 21, 1900.

And that's where part of the fascination comes in. Once released from prison, Matt completely abandoned his outlaw past, remarried, fathered two more children with his second wife, and settled into a peaceful, law-abiding existence. Dedicated to living an honest life, he earned the favor of lawmen and residents alike in his new home of Carbon County, Utah In fact, lawmen who had earlier wanted to see him behind bars for the rest of his life came to deeply respect him.

Matt Warner's badge; he served as deputy sheriff in Price.

Soon after settling in Carbon County, Matt ran for public office under his real name, Willard Erastus Christianson. He lost the election—no one knew who Willard Erastus Christianson *was*. He remedied that by legally changing his name to Matt Warner and running in the next election. He won handily, serving first as justice of the peace in Carbon County and then as the county's deputy sheriff.

That's right: a man who spent years as an outlaw was now the lawman. And his former criminal activities became an actual blessing.

Matt Warner served as justice of the peace and deputy sheriff in Price during his later life.

In his memoir, it explains that regardless of the situation, Matt never had to "resort to force of any kind or display his gun. He didn't have to." All that was necessary to maintain law and order, the memoir notes, was "a few mild hints or wisecracks from Matt Warner."[60] A fellow lawman noted that Matt was the most effective tax collector in the county: All he had to do was show up, knock on the door, and look the delinquent taxpayer in the face. No one wanted to flirt with disaster when it came to Matt Warner.

Toward the end of his life, Matt also worked as a detective and night guard in Price. He died a peaceful death of natural causes—rare among the outlaws of his day—in 1938, at the age of seventy-four. Just before his death his memoir, *The Last of the Bandit Riders*, was published in *Cosmopolitan* magazine. According to friends, he left out the best parts of the story to protect his old comrades and insisted that Butch Cassidy died in Argentina.[61]

The remains of his cabin are still standing in Levan.

CHAPTER FIVE
Elza Lay and Tom McCarty

IN THE LABYRINTH OF MORMON OUTLAWS who traversed the Utah Territory in the latter half of the nineteenth century, many crossed paths—with alarming frequency—and many moved from one loosely organized gang to another, hanging their hats wherever fortune seemed to be the most gracious. And that's not all: a surprising number were members of the same families, gathering fathers and sons and brothers and nephews into their carefully executed outlaw activities.

Two of those who seem to crop up often and in an astonishing range of places were Elza Lay, the gentle intellectual, and John Thomas ("Tom") McCarty, rumored to be the brains behind Butch Cassidy's boldest robberies.

Elza Lay

Some people garner fame because of their own deeds (or misdeeds, as the case may be). Others gain notoriety because of their associates. Outlaw Elza Lay falls solidly into that second category: His name went down in the history books not for anything he did on his own but because he was the best friend and partner in crime of Butch Cassidy, one of the American West's best-known bandits. And he's another outlaw who started out straight, fell into a life of crime when he mistakenly thought he killed someone, and eventually went straight again after a career of pretty remarkable capers.

Born William Ellsworth Lay on November 25, 1868, in Mount Pleasant, Ohio, he was one of three children of James Lander Lay and Mary Jane Bellew. Shortly after his birth the family moved to northeastern

Two mug shots of Elza Lay.

Colorado, where he grew up in a respectable, religious home. Not much is known about his childhood, but there is no evidence that he ever had even a minor scrape with the law. He was well educated in area schools and was also tutored at home by a refined, educated mother.

At the age of eighteen, he left home looking for adventure with his friend, William McGinnis. McGinnis—whose name Lay later used as an alias while working as a ranch hand—got homesick right away and returned home. Elza—the nickname coming from a shortened version of his middle name, Ellsworth—got a respectable job as the driver of a horse car in Denver.

Not unlike outlaw Matt Warner, Elza's criminal career began as the result of a misunderstanding. In fact, it actually stemmed from a gallant deed. While he was driving the horse car, an unruly man started harassing one of Elza's female passengers. After the man failed to heed several verbal warnings, eighteen-year-old Elza squared up his shoulders, set his jaw, and tossed the man from the car. The man landed unceremoniously on his head, and the impact rendered him unconscious.

Elza Lay in his early years.

Elza, erroneously believing he had killed the man, fled Denver to avoid being arrested and jailed.

His movements on the run aren't well documented, but we know he spent at least a few years in Texas working as a cowboy and ranch hand. It appears he began to migrate north with a herd of cattle but liked the Rocky Mountains so much he decided to stay. He eventually found his way to Baggs, Wyoming, a favorite gathering spot for outlaws and rustlers, where he hired on at the Calvert ranch. Theory is that he made many of his initial outlaw connections in Baggs and that he likely dabbled in some small-time rustling and other illegal activity while there. Elza was liked and respected by elements on both sides of the law; legitimate and law-abiding ranchers often fed him, loaned him cash, and even helped him evade arrest.

Elza (sometimes called Elzy) next popped up in 1889. He was living at Brown's Hole in Utah, where he landed a position as a ranch hand working for Matt Warner on Diamond Mountain—and where he came highly recommended by Brown's Hole rancher Charlie Crouse, for whom Elza had worked breaking horses. While he may have had at least a fleeting previous acquaintance with Butch Cassidy, they met up again and became lifelong friends at Brown's Hole. Part of that connection was fostered by romance: Elza was dating Josie Bassett, the daughter of a Brown's Hole rancher who supplied horses to the band of outlaws who frequented the Hole. At the same time, Butch was dating Josie's fifteen-year-old sister, Ann, who later became an outlaw herself.

Deciding his gig as a ranch hand wasn't paying well enough, Elza gave notice at the ranch, gathered up his earnings, and opened a gambling house in Vernal, just a hop, skip, and a jump from Brown's Hole. His outlaw friends were happy to support him, and business was booming. Elza was on his way to making a sizable profit when the establishment was shut down by the Uintah County sheriff.

With his business closed and nowhere else to turn, Elza went back to Brown's Hole, intending to resume his employment with Matt Warner, renew his friendship with Butch Cassidy, and rekindle his romantic interest in Josie Bassett. The job worked out. The romance did too—for a while. But Elza was disappointed to learn that Butch Cassidy had been arrested for stealing horses and was serving a two-year sentence in the Wyoming State Penitentiary in Rawlins.

Storefronts in Vernal, Utah, where Elza Lay opened a gambling house; the establishment was soon shut down by the Uintah County sheriff.

Restless but realizing his options were limited, Elza decided to bide his time at Brown's Hole until Butch was released from prison. His interest in Josie Bassett fizzled out, and he started dating a good Mormon girl named Maude Davis. Apparently he embraced both her and her faith. While Maude towed the religious line herself, she wasn't completely ignorant regarding outlawry—her brother, Albert Davis, was a small-time outlaw who liked to dance around the fringes of the law and who had committed a string of minor offenses in Wyoming.

When Butch was released from prison six months early for good behavior, he beat a path straight back to Brown's Hole. Elza couldn't wait to renew their friendship. Together, Butch and Elza built a cabin along the banks of the Green River and started scheming.

While Butch was known as the "gentleman" outlaw, Elza was the "academic," known for his intellectual curiosity, his love of learning, and his interest in literature, history, and pretty much every other educational subject. He was never found without a book in his saddlebags, and he was known to read by candlelight late into the night. His intellect was so keen that some think he was actually the "brains" behind many of Butch's capers: Elza, some say, came up with the plans down to the most minute detail, then Butch exercised the bravado to carry them out.

During the first half of 1896, Butch started gathering a gang of outlaws he would rely on for the next five or so years. Called "the Wild Bunch," they were headed up by Butch himself; because his former partner, Matt Warner, was in jail, Elza became second in command—a position he maintained even after Warner surfaced again.

The first heist Butch and Elza pulled off together was actually done to help a friend: One of a handful of men legitimately hired to intimidate two prospectors who were trying to steal a mining claim, Matt Warner found himself in serious trouble. Intending only to browbeat the men into abandoning their efforts, Matt was unprepared when the argument suddenly erupted into gunfight. In the ensuing shootout, the two prospectors were killed, and Matt and two others were arrested and held in an Ogden jail. To his dying day, Matt claimed he shot in self-defense. Desperate for help, he sent word to his close friend Butch Cassidy that he needed an attorney.

Attorneys were expensive in those days but it didn't take Butch long to figure out a quick solution. He set his sights on the bank in Montpelier, Idaho—one he figured would be an easy mark. Butch asked Elza and a third friend, Bub Meeks, to help. On August 13, 1896, after weeks of meticulous planning, the three sat at a table in a nearby saloon, waiting for the perfect moment to strike.

That perfect moment occurred when, just before closing time, the cashier ambled out of the bank to talk to a friend on the sidewalk. Without revealing their guns, Elza and Butch, wearing bandanas over the lower half of their faces, ordered the cashier back into the bank, forced everyone inside against the wall, and scooped up more than $7,100—today's equivalent of $136,000—in cash, gold, and silver. Meeks, also sporting a bandana, stayed outside with the getaway horses. And get away they did: By the time the posse was organized, Butch and his companions were on their second set of fresh horses and putting miles between them and the law. After a week on the hoof, the posse simply gave up the pursuit.

Two weeks later, Butch delivered $16,000 in cash to Rock Springs attorney Douglas Preston, who took on Matt Warner's defense. It was Elza's first "big" job, and he felt justified. After all, the money was being used to help their friend who had been wrongly incarcerated for shooting in self-defense.

Uneasy about returning to their cabin on the Green River, Butch and Elza gathered up girlfriends Ann Bassett and Maude Davis and set up housekeeping in the rugged Robbers' Roost area. While Butch remained single, Elza married Maude—likely not an altogether pleasant prospect for her devout Mormon parents. After all, this was not the priesthood-honoring, covenant-keeping boy most Mormon parents dreamed of marrying their daughters. No one wants a son-in-law whose mug shot is peppered all over "Wanted" posters.

By early April 1897 Butch and Elza were planning their boldest robbery ever, and they sent the women back to Green River for safekeeping. By then Maude was pregnant with Elza's first child, and she demanded that he abandon his outlaw lifestyle and settle down.

Elza refused.

And so it was that on April 21, 1897, while Maude was brooding in Green River, Elza and Butch robbed the Pleasant Valley Coal Company payroll—all $8,000 of it (more than $150,000 in today's currency)—in Castle Gate, Utah. It was astonishingly easy: Elza sat casually on his horse, holding another horse and looking like he was just waiting for a

Castle Gate, Utah, where Elza Lay and Butch Cassidy staged their most spectacular robbery, that of the Pleasant Valley Coal Company payroll.

friend. Butch sat on a chair against the wall, his hat pulled low; passersby undoubtedly thought he was catching a snooze in the warm sun. But all that changed the second the paymaster emerged from the train with the bag of cash. Butch leaped forward, shoved a gun in the paymaster's ribs, yanked the bag away from him, and tossed it to Elza before leaping on his own horse. A third accomplice several miles away sliced the telegraph cables so the law couldn't alert authorities up the line.

With a respectable head start and a volley of fresh horses stationed along the way, Elza and Butch made it to Robbers' Roost and disappeared from sight before the pursuing posses actually engaged in a shootout with each other at Buckhorn Wash. Each mistook the other for the outlaws.

A few months later, Maude gave birth to Elza's daughter, Marvel. Again, Maude insisted that Elza turn his back on outlawry, settle down, and live a respectable life worthy of a husband and father.

Again, Elza refused.

Over the next two years, Elza and Butch moved first to New Mexico—where they worked briefly on a ranch—and then headed north to Wyoming, where they committed the most famous of their train robberies. On June 2, 1899, the Wild Bunch held up the Overland Flyer train near Wilcox, Wyoming; their take was more than $60,000—almost $1.2 million in today's currency—a handsome profit even considering it had to be divided among all participating members of the Wild Bunch. When the pursuing posse engaged the gang in a shootout, Wild Bunch outlaw Kid Curry killed Converse County sheriff Josiah Hazen, but none of the Wild Bunch took a bullet. They successfully escaped into the Hole-in-the-Wall then temporarily scattered until the law cooled off.

Just a month later the gang struck again when they robbed a Rio Grande train on July 11, 1899, near Folsom, New Mexico. Butch masterminded the heist but was not directly involved in it, which means that Elza led three other outlaws in the actual robbery. Under Elza's leadership, the four escaped with their biggest payoff ever, getting an unprecedented $70,000 (equivalent to $1.33 million today). Using their tried-and-true getaway method, the four headed for New Mexico.

Things didn't go as well this time, though. Lawmen were determined to help the railroad recover the stolen loot and pursued the gang in a well-led posse under the direction of Huerfano Colorado County

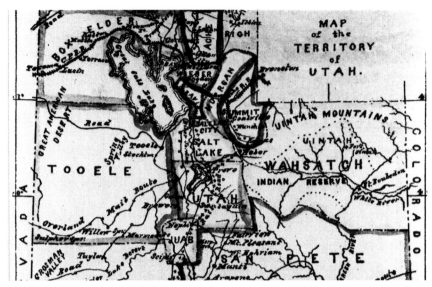

Elza Lay's outlaw career eventually focused almost exclusively on train robbery, a crime that netted a much higher profit with significantly less risk of capture.

sheriff Ed Farr. Within a few days, Farr and his posse cornered the outlaws at an area known as Turkey Creek; in the subsequent shootout, Doña Ana County deputy Kent Kearney was wounded. He died the next day. A second deputy was shot and seriously wounded, as was Wild Bunch outlaw Sam Ketchum.

The gang managed to evade capture, even with the daunting challenge of dragging the wounded Sam Ketchum, and fled into the surrounding hills. But this time the posse didn't give up so quickly; after all, one of their own had been gunned down. On July 16, the outlaws were again cornered in the Turkey Creek area and a second shootout erupted. This time luck ran thin for both the gang and the lawmen who pursued them. Elza shot and killed Sheriff Farr and wounded Colfax County deputy Henry Love, who died a few days later from his wounds. Elza also took a few bullets but managed to escape with two of the other outlaws. The already-wounded Sam Ketchum was unable to get away and was captured by members of the posse; he died in custody from the wounds sustained in the shootout.

Elza Lay now had a murder rap on his head, and it wasn't just any murder: He had killed a sheriff and a deputy. He managed to lay low for a few weeks, but when he went into Carlsbad, New Mexico, for supplies on August 16, he was cornered and captured. Charged with not only the robbery but the killings, he was convicted and sentenced to life in prison, a term he would serve in the New Mexico State Penitentiary.

First it was Matt Warner. Now it was Elza Lay—the second "right-hand man" Butch Cassidy had lost to a lengthy prison sentence. Butch made repeated attempts to secure amnesty for Elza from the governor of Utah, but the governor turned a deaf ear because of the string of robberies and killings committed by the Wild Bunch. Besides, the governor argued, this one was squarely in the lap of New Mexico, not Utah. With Elza, they had finally managed to put one of the kingpins behind bars. And they intended to keep him there.

Meanwhile, back on the ranch (literally), the whole thing was simply too much for Maude, who had consistently pleaded with Elza to fly straight. Maude gathered up Marvel and filed for divorce.

During the seven years he spent in prison, Elza mellowed. His good behavior earned him a job as a trustee to the warden, which indirectly led to his release. In his role as trustee, he often accompanied the warden, and one memorable jaunt took them to Santa Fe. They returned to a horrific scenario: The inmates—some of whom were exceptionally violent—had taken the warden's wife and daughter hostage inside the prison. Elza entered the prison, reasoned with the inmates, and was able to convince them to release both women.

To reward Elza for his heroism, New Mexico governor Miguel Antonio Otero pardoned him on January 10, 1906. At least that's how it appeared on the official record. Behind the scenes, it seems the governor had been working on a pardon—or at least a parole—for some time. Why? A little on the greedy side, he was intensely interested in gold, and Elza had hinted that he knew of some potentially lucrative gold veins hidden away in Utah's Ute Indian territory. In fact, Elza manufactured a plausible-sounding story about having worked as a guard for a well-known gold miner. He even arranged for Matt Warner—by then out of prison—to send an official-looking "map" of the area. A good friend of the warden, Governor Otero convinced the warden to go in on a deal: together, they would raise the capital to launch the gold venture, and Elza would provide the direction and know-how. To make it all happen, the governor would somehow arrange a pardon. The rescue

Shot of an early gold mine. Elza Lay secured a pardon based on the promise he could lead the warden to a lucrative gold mine.

of the warden's wife and daughter provided the perfect opportunity for that pardon. When the prison doors were locked on January 10, Elza found himself on the outside with a little cash in his pocket and an order to find the lost gold mine.

The mine, of course, never materialized.

It was over. Seven years behind bars had convinced Elza that a life of crime was really no life at all; now divorced and permanently separated from his daughter, he headed back to Baggs, Wyoming, a place where he felt at least a little at home. Baggs had been a longtime hangout for mostly minor outlaws, but Elza was determined to avoid that life. Other than a single rumored visit with Josie and Ann Bassett, Elza had no contact with his cronies from the Wild Bunch after his release from prison.

That was really a fairly easy task. After all, the major figures from the outlaw gang were pretty much dead and gone. While Elza was cooling his heels behind bars, Butch Cassidy and the Sundance Kid went to South America and never openly returned. Ben Kilpatrick and Laura Bullion were captured in Knoxville, Tennessee, and thrown behind bars. Kid Curry was killed during a shootout with Colorado lawmen, and Utah lawmen killed George "Flat Nosed" Curry as he fled the scene of a crime. It was a good time to make a clean break, and that's exactly what Elza decided to do.

In Baggs, Elza met Mary Calvert, whose father owned the Calvert ranch where Elza had worked in his youth; three years later they married and subsequently raised two children. After working with only moderate success as a gold miner and saloon owner, Elza turned to oil exploration. A previous interest had caused him to study geology in some detail, and he eventually discovered some oil deposits near Ogden, Utah, as well as the Hiawatha Oil Fields in Wyoming.

Elza was skilled at *finding* oil, but the oil business was risky and unstable. Within a few years, he had lost all his assets and was forced to find something else to do.

Elza had the skills to make a quick dollar as an outlaw, but even with poverty staring him in the face he resisted the temptation to return to his old ways. He and Mary took their family to Southern California, where he supervised the building of the Colorado River aqueduct system in an area just north of the Mexico border. His last job was as water master for the Imperial Valley Irrigation Company in southern California.

He managed to stay away from even the most minor criminal activity and became a devoted family man, respected in his community. On November 10, 1934, Elza died of a heart attack in Los Angeles—far from the way most of his old associates died in a hail of gunfire. He is buried at Forest Lawn Cemetery in Glendale, California.

John Thomas ("Tom") McCarty

Tom McCarty was another outlaw whose fame is pretty firmly fastened onto that of others. In his case, it was Butch Cassidy and Matt Warner, two of the most notorious of the Mormon outlaws.

Tom—a Mormon himself—was born and raised on a ranch in Ephraim. His association with Matt Warner actually started fairly early in his life when he married

Outlaw John Thomas ("Tom") McCarty, who eventually led his father, brother, and nephew into lives of crime.

Matt's sister, Christina ("Tennie"), a good Mormon girl who grew up in the Christianson home in Levan. Before it was all over, Tom would become Matt's most trusted mentor and would lead his own father and brother into a life of outlawry.

Not long after Tom and Tennie got married, Tom took an interest in his young brother-in-law's career . . . criminal career, that is. Tom and his brother Bill had started a ranch near Cortez, Colorado, and had been rustling and robbing cattle throughout the eastern Utah Territory since 1884. Tom was eager to pass on the tricks of the trade to Matt—after all, he was family. As it turned out, Tom had a willing pupil in Matt, who eagerly took instruction in how to rustle cattle, steal horses, and shoot a gun. Before long, Tom and Bill included Matt in their capers, and they became known throughout the territory as "the Invincible Trio."

During that same stretch of time, Matt had been working with race horses on Charlie Crouse's ranch in Brown's Hole. When he decided to temporarily abandon his own ranch on Diamond Mountain and go on the race circuit with his horse, Betty, he entered

Tom McCarty and his brother, Bill, initially ran a cattle ranch near Cortez, Colorado, much like this one, where they headquartered their cattle rustling operations.

a race in Telluride, Colorado, that would change his life. It was at the Telluride race that he agreed to a bet with nineteen-year-old ore hauler Butch Cassidy. Butch loved horses, fancied the thrill of a race, and wagered that his horse could outrun Betty. No such luck: Betty handily won the race, and Butch saw an opportunity to escape the dull world of hauling ore. When he expressed real interest in the hardscrabble life of riding the circuit, it didn't take long for Matt and Butch to become partners in the race enterprise—and, in the bargain, to form a lifelong friendship.

Matt and Butch had enviable skills with horses—and Betty herself was invincible. She won every race in which she ran; word spread, and soon area cowboys tired of losing their money. No one but Indians would agree to race their horses against Betty. With lack of profitable competition putting a damper on their racing venture, Matt and Butch ended up in Cortez, where they located the ranch belonging to Matt's brothers-in-law, Tom and Bill McCarty.

It was a long-overdue and happy reunion, but there was only so much at the isolated ranch to capture the imagination of four restless outlaws. With too much time on their hands, the rigors of a remote location, and an all-but-dead racing circuit, the four spent plenty of hours talking about the lure of easy money. By then Tom McCarty had a voracious gambling habit, and he needed money. Lots of it. The easier, the better. One thing led to another, and the enticement of big money helped Tom easily cast aside his religious upbringing. Cattle rustling—so common that even some of the mainstream Mormons occasionally participated—just wasn't lucrative enough anymore. Horse stealing really didn't cut it either. Instead, Tom and his three companions spent nights around the campfire planning bank robberies.

The prospect was tantalizing. They came up with what seemed like surefire tactics and were antsy to try them out. And on March 30, 1889, the rubber finally hit the road, so to speak.

That Saturday morning, a fastidiously dressed Tom McCarty strolled casually into the First National Bank of Denver; sporting full-length trousers and a knee-length coat, he blended in easily with the most affluent bank customers as he asked to see bank president David Moffat. Completely unconcerned, Moffat approached McCarty with an easy smile.

McCarty, still possessed of the manners of his youth, smiled back then politely stated, "Excuse me, sir, but I just overheard a plot to rob this bank."

His expression moving from courtesy to alarm, Moffat was concerned. "How on earth did you learn of this plot?" he asked.

"I planned it," McCarty quietly responded, producing a pistol. "Put up your hands." With the terrified Moffat's arms in the air, McCarty next produced a bottle of colorless, oily liquid that he claimed was nitroglycerine—an explosive more powerful than black powder. "Give me $21,000 in cash," McCarty purred, "or I'll blow this bank—and you with it—sky-high."

Moffat didn't have to be asked twice. With rapid-fire precision, he retrieved $21,000—the equivalent of nearly $400,000 in today's currency—from the head teller and thrust the bundle at McCarty, careful to avoid the bottle of reputed explosive. With a quiet "thank-you," McCarty strolled out of the bank, handed the loot to an accomplice on the sidewalk, and both easily vanished into the bustling Denver crowd. Shaken, Moffat was powerless to pursue the two.

The robbery made sensational newspaper headlines, but no one at the time knew the identity of the well-dressed robber or his mysterious accomplice. Only later did it become known that Tom McCarty himself was the fashionable thief and Matt Warner his brazen co-conspirator.

It was almost too easy for the pair to believe. With little effort and out nothing more than a suit of fine clothing and a bottle of liquid (almost certainly *not* nitroglycerine), the two had made off with a very respectable haul. And they had done it in a major city to boot. And none of the accounts mention a gun even being fired.

Guns *were* used in the next heist—as was Butch Cassidy, who apparently wasn't involved in the Denver robbery. Buoyed by the easy success of the Denver job, the trio set their sights on the San Miguel National Bank in the small but wealthy mining town of Telluride, Colorado. The Telluride robbery was the first—but definitely not the last—major crime to involve Butch Cassidy.

The robbery was planned down to the smallest detail by Tom McCarty himself, who would apparently be the brainchild of many future Wild Bunch operations. It was the first robbery to employ relay horses and fresh water stationed along the route, giving the outlaws a solid head start ahead of any pursuing posse. And it was the first

Tom McCarty's name inscribed on a rock at a spring near present-day Monticello, Utah, not far from Robbers' Roost.

robbery to involve the kingpins of the Wild Bunch, Butch Cassidy's famous gang.

In order to participate in the robbery, Butch and Matt quit their nearly yearlong jobs on a ranch owned by Harry Adsit. But the two didn't let Adsit in on the fact that they were leaving for good—instead, Butch said he merely needed to visit family in Utah. As a gift for the hard-working cowboy, for whom he had developed real affection, Adsit gave Butch two of the finest four-year-old horses he had broken. Adsit then waved his hat in what he believed to be a temporary farewell to Butch, Matt, and Tom McCarty.

But Butch didn't saddle up and head toward home. Instead, he, Matt, and Tom rode into Telluride on the morning of Saturday, June 22, 1889. It was a meticulous plan. Tom had spent a fair amount of time in Telluride and knew he'd be recognized, so he focused on working with his horses—a seemingly innocent pastime. Matt, a stranger to Telluride, mingled with people in town, learning names and occupations and engaging in a poker game or two. As for Butch, he settled in at a table in the saloon across the street from the bank and kept a sharp eye on the habits of the bank personnel.

With everything in place, they were ready. On the morning of Monday, June 24, 1889, the three casually rode up to the bank at a slow clip. Tom stayed outside, again busying himself with the horses. At 10 A.M. sharp, just as county clerk Charles Painter left the bank, the other two outlaws walked in.

Inside, as had been observed over the previous two days, head teller C. Hyde was counting the cash—and didn't even see what was about to hit him. Matt shoved his pistol into Hyde's face and demanded the cash he'd been so carefully counting. Shocked by an attack he hadn't seen coming and terrified for his life, Hyde swept the cash into a bag and thrust it at Matt.

But that wasn't the end of it. As Tom stayed outside priming the getaway horses, Matt held a gun on Hyde while Butch jumped behind the cage and filled several sacks, emptying the counter and the vault of its currency and gold. By the time the two were headed for the door, they had scooped up approximately $21,000—nearly $400,000 in today's currency.

Tom then flew into action. Shouting from his position outside the door, Tom invited Hyde to stay put and keep quiet or die. He then shot at the feet of the teller as extra incentive to obey orders.

The three galloped at full speed away from the bank, shooting their pistols in random directions to intimidate the people on the street. They weren't immediately pursued by law enforcement for several reasons. For one thing, Butch had cut a deal with the town marshal, Jim Clark, who agreed to be out of town during the actual robbery. They left Clark's share of the money in a hollow log outside of town and galloped away as fast as they could force the horses. For another, their well-planned system of stationing fresh horses at relay stations gave them a thirty-five-mile head start on the posse that did eventually pursue them.

Even though Tom McCarty had spent a fair amount of time in Telluride, even he wasn't recognized at first. In fact, the robbery was initially blamed on a different gang. On June 26, 1889, the *Rocky Mountain News* reported, "The robbery of the San Miguel Valley bank of Telluride by four daring cowboys of the Stockton outfit on the Mancos is one of the boldest affairs in Colorado."

And that's where things get interesting. Tom McCarty was a known entity in town, but the other two may have remained anonymous had it not been for one thing: rancher Harry Adsit happened to be riding

The Book Cliffs, where Tom McCarty escaped following his bank robbery in Telluride.

toward town to stock up on supplies as the outlaws flew by in the other direction. He was shocked to see Butch—after all, Butch should have been at his family's ranch in Utah by then. By the time the posse started out and encountered Adsit, they enlisted his help in pursuing the outlaws. Adsit's effort was halfhearted at best, and the trio escaped with the loot.

Immediately following the robbery, news reports expressed confidence in the capture of the people responsible for the heist. An article in the *Salt Lake Herald* stated a common sentiment: "It is more than probable that they will be captured before 24 hours." As a matter of fact, they were not captured within twenty-four hours—or at all.

The three outlaws ended up in Robbers' Roost, but it was definitely not as the crow flies—and wasn't the easy getaway some believed it to be.[62] According to historian Richard Patterson, the trio crossed the Colorado River into Utah on a ferry near Moab, where they had several close encounters with a local posse. They managed to escape through the current-day Arches National Park to the foot of the Book Cliffs near current-day Thompson Springs. From there, the three headed north, galloping at full speed for Brown's Hole, where they hid out on Diamond Mountain in a cabin owned by their old friend, rancher Charlie Crouse.

They may have stayed in Crouse's cabin longer, but Crouse sent one of his ranch hands to warn the trio that a posse had arrived at Brown's Hole looking for them. It was common practice in the Hole for the law-abiding ranchers to "protect" the outlaws, many of whom were considered personal friends. And so Tom, Butch, and Matt received the warning and rode as hard as they could for Robbers' Roost, hiding by day and traveling by night. They managed to evade the posse, and none of the three was ever arrested for the robbery. Butch Cassidy's younger brother was later arrested for other crimes while bringing supplies to the trio; he was put in prison for the former crimes.

Why did Tom's expert planning take the outlaws north to Brown's Hole when Robbers' Roost was much closer to Telluride—and a superior natural fortress as well? Richard Patterson thinks Tom directed them to Brown's Hole first "because they knew that the authorities would guess they would head to the Roost and cut them off before they could get there. Or maybe they choose not to hide in the Roost because of its heat—only a desperate man would try to live off the Roost in July and August."[63]

It was time to split up, and the three went their separate ways for a time to throw off their scent. Accounts are varied but highly diverse about how Tom McCarty spent that time. Some say he participated in minor criminal activity, such as rustling. Some say he participated in the robbery of a bank in Montpelier, Idaho—a robbery staged by Butch Cassidy, Elza Lay, and Bub Meeks to get the money needed for Matt Warner's defense attorney. In actuality, Tom McCarty was in California at the time of the robbery, though rumors are that he was the brains behind the job.

We do know that the group eventually joined back up and wandered into Wyoming, where Butch Cassidy decided to stay. Tom had other plans. He enlisted his brother Bill, who had been a regular partner in Tom's exploits, and his nephew Fred and headed northwest with Matt Warner to Washington, where his father, George, had moved years earlier. Things hadn't been that great in Ephraim for the McCarty family, so George had purchased a ranch first in Oregon and then

Tom McCarty's brother, Bill, who joined him in many of his outlaw activities.

in Washington and had been eking out a rugged existence there. The outlaws decided to settle in for a breather and started helping out on the ranch.

But things weren't very prosperous in Washington, either, so it didn't take much arm-twisting for Tom to persuade his father that there was an easier—and faster—way to make a buck. With Tom's careful planning, the group robbed a bank in nearby Roslyn of $20,000—the equivalent of almost $400,000 in today's currency. Lawmen made a furious attempt to capture the outlaws but were unsuccessful—at least initially.

The McCarty men were flying high with the thrill of the conquest, but Matt Warner, now a new father, was rethinking things. He made a solemn promise to his young wife: within a few days, he said, he would take his share of the Roslyn funds, dig up the rest of his stash, leave the McCarty gang, and make a fresh start with his new family. Somehow, he said, he'd find a legitimate way to earn a living.

But no sooner had the promise been uttered than Matt was arrested for the Roslyn heist. And he'd barely had time to warm up his jail cell before Tom's father, George, was unceremoniously tossed in the same cell. For whatever reason, the other three—Tom, his brother Bill, and his nephew Fred—were never arrested.

Tom sent a lawyer to the jail to see what could be done to free his father and Matt. The lawyer, clearly not an outstanding model of ethical behavior, told Matt the pair could be freed if they put enough money in the right hands. Desperate to see daylight and make good on his promise to his wife, Matt drew a map to the exact spot where his stash was buried—all $41,000 of it (almost $800,000 in today's currency). He told the lawyer to take whatever he needed in order to spring the two from jail.

Time ticked by, and the two made an unsuccessful escape attempt. Then suddenly jailers unlocked the cell door and George and Matt were set free. Imagine Matt's shock when he found the lawyer had taken his entire $41,000 fortune to "buy" the pair's freedom. When confronted, the lawyer handed over $500 as a "goodwill" gesture, moaning that it came out of his own pocket.

That was enough for Matt. Though he was later jailed for killing a man in self-defense, he avoided any more criminal behavior and eventually became a deputy sheriff and justice of the peace.

Not so with Tom McCarty. While details are sketchy, he spent the next three or four years committing a series of bank and train robberies, aided and abetted by, at various times, his brother and his nephew. Other members of the Wild Bunch may have been involved as well. There is also evidence that members of the group spent various stints behind bars during those years.

On Thursday, September 7, 1893—less than two months after being released from jail for an earlier crime—the three committed what would be their final robbery as a team. Nephew Fred stayed outside the Farmers and Merchants Bank in Denver with the horses to maintain a lookout while his father, Bill, and his uncle Tom rushed into the bank and demanded cash. It was a brazen robbery, committed in broad daylight in front of several dozen witnesses, and didn't seem to bear the marks of Tom's usual careful planning.

And from there, things went terribly wrong.

Cashier A. T. Blachey—co-owner of the bank—began to shout for help as soon as the outlaws made their demand. In an attempt to quiet the teller, Tom leaped over the railing and rammed his pistol into Blachey's ribs. In the meantime, Bill started cramming as much cash as he could find into a large sack.

If it had ended there, no one would have been seriously hurt. But Tom McCarty had not counted on a gang of law-abiding, armed men who were determined to protect their town.

Suddenly Fred burst into the bank with unexpected news: A crowd was gathering outside, and some of them were armed. All of a sudden Tom's plans underwent an abrupt change. In the ensuing commotion, the outlaws started shooting; Blachey was killed and his assistant teller was seriously wounded.

What happened next occurred in rapid-fire succession. The three outlaws rushed out of the bank and mounted their horses, hoping against hope for a clean escape. Simultaneously, nearby hardware merchant Ray Simpson had heard the commotion, grabbed a new repeating rifle off his store shelves, and loaded it as he ran into the street. His timing was perfect: He raised the rifle just as the trio galloped past and managed to plant a slug in Bill McCarty's head, knocking him out of his saddle.

Bill's spooked horse kept galloping; Fred did an abrupt about-face and dismounted to help his dying father. By the time the dust settled, both father and son had been shot to death; their bodies were riddled with bullets. United in life, they were also united in death: Lawmen roped the two bodies together and propped them up against the wall of the bank as a statement to anyone else who might have thought about staging a robbery. From there, they were dragged to an undertaker. The entire take from the robbery—a mere $700 (a little more than $13,000 in today's equivalent)—was found on the bodies and was recovered.

As for Tom, he kept riding—as hard and fast as he could—even though he had been severely wounded. Mostly because of the commotion surrounding his companions, he was able to evade the pursuing posse. Where he ended up, and whether he eventually survived his wounds, is unknown. From all accounts, his outlaw days had come to an end.

Tom McCarty simply dropped off the radar—something he has in common with another infamous Mormon outlaw, David Lant.

David Barnabas Lant, born in Payson, Utah, became part of one of the most notorious twosomes in outlaw history and was known for his daring prison and jail escapes.

CHAPTER SIX
David Lant

IF YOU HAVEN'T HEARD OF outlaw David Lant, you're not alone.

Unlike Butch Cassidy, his is not a household name. In fact, his own highly respected Mormon family rarely whispered his name in *its* household, even generations later. Only after a safe hundred years or so had passed did one of their number step forward with even the sketchiest of information.

Truth be told, they were just too embarrassed.

As with so many Mormon outlaws, he was a good boy who grew up in a respectable, religious home but who had a temper and got involved with the "wrong crowd" as an adolescent. He fathered a son with girlfriend Annie Boulton before her outraged father ran David out of town rather than let him marry her. One thing led to another, and before long—as with so many of the other outlaws—he felt he'd sunk too far below his traditional Mormon values to ever be redeemed. The die was cast.

David Lant is one of very few Mormon outlaws of the day who never associated with—or even knew—Butch Cassidy, though he may have taken a few random rides with the Wild Bunch. While many of the other Mormon outlaws were branded as "gentlemen" outlaws, he definitely did not fit that description. His crimes ranged all the way from simple drunken brawls to cold-blooded murder, and everything in between, but he is best remembered as an escape artist. He never worried about the length of a prison sentence because he never met a jail that could effectively hold him for long.

But perhaps the most unique thing about David Lant was the fact that he simply vanished. Literally. The earth might as well have swallowed him up. There are lots of stories about where he might have gone and what he might have done, but none has been substantiated. He was, as historian Douglas W. Ellison dubbed him in a biographical work, "the vanished outlaw." His was not a lifestyle "conducive to freedom or survival," wrote Ellison, but "in the end, Dave Lant got clean away."[64]

An article in the March 10, 1898, *Salt Lake Tribune* summed up the dichotomy of a small-town Mormon boy gone wrong. When twenty-four-year-old Lant was captured and charged with murder after a nearly yearlong, highly publicized manhunt, the *Tribune* reported from Payson:

> David Lant is a boy born and raised here and who has failed to accept good advice from his father by the same name, and who greatly mourns for the actions of his wayward son. Nothing has been allowed to creep into the press news from here on account of Lant's respectable relatives.
>
> David is not, or rather was not, considered a bad young man. He gradually strayed from the path of rectitude by one small petty crime then another, until his associations led him so far he could not return. He went lower and lower into crime until the penitentiary was reached, from whence he made his escape and joined the outlaws. It is still hoped that he will not be lynched before he has a chance to be the prodigal son and return to his glad father, repent and abandon such a reckless life.[65]

Born September 14, 1874, in Payson, Utah, David Barnabas Lant was the fourth of nine children and oldest son of David T. Lant and Elsie Tanner Lant, stalwart community and Mormon Church leaders. Not unlike Butch Cassidy, David came from sturdy pioneer stock that had been valiantly faithful to the Church.

A look at outlaw David Lant's pioneer heritage helps set the stage for an oddly amazing story. Let's start with his father. After seven years of being on his own, he ended up in a Liverpool boardinghouse where he fell in love with his much-older landlady. On February 25, 1850, nineteen-year-old old David Lant married forty-one-year-old Elizabeth

Harding, a widow who had a daughter not much younger than David. Within two years, all three were baptized members of the Church, and in 1855 they headed to Zion as part of the Milo Andrus Company. Despite having only one arm, the result of an accident involving a train, David took charge of his family, walked much of the way to the Salt Lake Valley, and drove a herd of cattle in front of him. He was ordained to the forty-fifth Quorum of the Seventy in 1857.

He and Elizabeth pulled up stakes and moved fifteen miles south to Payson, where he would enter a plural marriage to Elsie Tanner, a girl whose family had joined the Church near Kirtland. An avid doctrinal expert, he became a popular speaker in the wards and stakes surrounding his home. His wives shared his interest in all things doctrinal, and young David Lant, who was baptized at the age of eight, spent hours at his mother's knee as she told stories from the Bible and the Book of Mormon.

Federal officials were hot on the tail of polygamists at the time, but the Lant family seemed to escape persecution—probably because David Lant's first wife was old enough to be his mother and none of the officials even suspected they might be married. After thirty-seven years of marriage, she died in Payson at the age of seventy-eight. Less than a year later, David's second wife, Elsie, died of dropsy and heart disease at the age of thirty-eight. Many feel that his mother's early death—when he was only fourteen—had at least some influence on David Lant's eventual career as an outlaw.

Just six days later, David's father married again—this time to a stern, ill-humored woman from Scotland named Elizabeth Luke, who had been married twice before and whose only infant child had previously died. Feeling no affection for this new stepmother, David and the other children addressed her only as Mrs. Luke. (Some feel that the punitive, unfeeling stepmother might have also influenced young David's eventual outlaw behavior.)

During those years in Payson under the formidable gaze of his Scottish stepmother, David started dabbling in mischievous shenanigans—pranks that were certainly harmless enough but that likely set the tone for what would become a lifetime of outlaw behavior. But David also apparently had a sensitive, artistic side as well and was known to spontaneously compose fine poetry.

After David Lant left home, Waldemar "Wal" Lybbert taught him how to shear sheep and tried to mentor him in an honest way of earning a living.

No one knows whether his severe and unyielding stepmother was to blame, but within two years of his father's marriage to Elizabeth Luke, David left home. While there aren't many details of exactly where David went after leaving, he did manage to keep in occasional touch with his family back in Payson. He apparently worked fairly steadily as a sheepherder, most of the time in and around Vernal. He was known as a strong and good worker, reliable and steady. Vernal area resident Waldemar "Wal" Lybbert—later to become part of the posse that would doggedly hunt Lant and his partners in crime—was the one to mentor David, teaching him how to shear sheep.

Once he left home, David—nursing a rebellious streak that caused him to cast aside many of his Mormon codes of conduct—became a heavy drinker, something that would have shocked his conservative family back in Payson. In early 1897, his drinking led to his first serious brush with the law and landed his name in a *Vernal Express* headline, though the newspaper inaccurately reported his last name as "Lance."

It all happened on the morning of Thursday, February 4, 1897, at the Exchange Saloon in Vernal, a respectable, "first-class" drinking establishment that served rare whiskeys for twenty-five cents a drink and pedaled the finest brands of imported cigars. Sometime between eleven-thirty and noon, an already-drunk and agitated David Lant staggered into the saloon looking for trouble.

And trouble is exactly what he found. Within minutes after twenty-two-year-old David landed on a stool at the bar, he launched into an abusive verbal tirade against James McNaughton, almost twice his age and one of the proprietors of the lavish saloon. Seeing that David was drunk, McNaughton simply ignored him and went on with his work. But that didn't stop David, who responded by getting louder and more obnoxious as the minutes ticked by.

When McNaughton got up and started to walk past David, the young drunk suddenly picked up a full liquor bottle and slammed it into McNaughton's head, gashing his scalp wide open and knocking him against a pool table. At that instant, things went rapidly downhill.

When the inebriated David reached into his coat pocket for another liquor bottle—his weapon of choice that day—McNaughton's co-proprietor, William McCaslin, assumed David was reaching for a gun. He rapidly pulled out his own pistol and started firing in David's direction. The first two shots missed. The third burrowed through Lant's left shoulder, perilously close to his heart, and exited under his arm.

Anesthetized by a liberal dose of alcohol, Lant didn't seem to realize he'd

been shot. Still in a drunken stupor, he staggered out of the saloon, hopped on his horse, and rode away. He was found a few minutes later a short distance down the road, disoriented, his shirt soaked with blood. A Good Samaritan rushed him off for medical help. No criminal charges were filed against him. He forgave McCaslin for shooting him, chalking the incident up to a simple misunderstanding.

Sketch of David Lant in his prison stripes.

After the Vernal saloon incident, a slightly shaken David laid low for six months, possibly doing odd jobs for local sheepherders. During that time it seems he also made some new friends, not the sort of which his parents would have approved. In August 1897, he showed up in the little hamlet of Woodruff, Utah, northwest of Vernal and just a few miles from the Wyoming border, with two pals—both of whom were older seasoned criminals and both of whom had used a variety of aliases. One, a twenty-nine-year-old native of Salt Lake City who was "raised a Mormon," called himself William Johnson. The other, a twenty-four-year-old Iowa native, called himself Charles Ferguson and had formerly lived for a time in Woodruff.

On the evening of August 19, 1897, the three silently let themselves into one of Woodruff's leading business establishments: the Cook Brothers General Mercantile. The intrepid trio decided to get their duds for free, outfitting themselves with everything from a full set of new underwear all the way to shoes, gloves, hats, and ties.

The next morning Rich County sheriff Daniel Sinclair Marshall was on the case, and he figured the three transients from Vernal had pulled off the theft. Within hours he had cuffed the three outlaws and dragged them to the Rich County justice of the peace, ten miles down the road in Randolph. The other two were arrested as William Johnson and Charles Ferguson; in a day before positive ID was required at every turn, Lant reported his name as David Jones, most likely to spare his respectable family in Payson the negative publicity.

Officials were convinced of the guilt of all three, but there were two major problems. First, none had any of the stolen merchandise—not even so much as a tie pin. Hard to make charges stick when there's no stolen property. Second, all three provided credible-sounding alibis for each other. When all was said and done, Justice Joseph H. Neville had no choice but to set them free.

Neville was frustrated by the turn of events and went on his own personal vendetta: He decided to stalk the outlaws and catch them red-handed with the merchandise. It didn't take long for his instincts to prove right. Late the next afternoon, peering through a set of field glasses, he saw the three remove the stolen clothing from a hiding place, mount their horses, and gallop hard and fast for the Wyoming border, about ten miles away.

Neville immediately reported his find to Sheriff Marshall, who was fast on the tail of the outlaws; although in hard pursuit, he reached Evanston, Wyoming—roughly twenty-two miles away—without being able to overtake his quarry. At Evanston Marshall gathered reinforcements: the sheriff of Uinta County and an Evanston city constable. After resting for the night, they continued their pursuit on Sunday, August 22.

About fifteen miles outside Evanston they found what they were looking for: the three were casually enjoying dinner at the roadside, their horses tied to a wagon belonging to an older man, Henry Sellon, who had been on his way home to Fort Bridger. The trio had erroneously believed they had gone far enough to evade pursuit or capture; though heavily armed, they surrendered to lawmen without resistance. And there in the bed of Sellon's wagon was the missing merchandise, down to the last tie pin.

Sellon, an innocent bystander, was sent on his way, and officials returned the three prisoners—described in the local paper as "three tough looking customers"—to Randolph, where they were tossed behind bars to await their second hearing before Justice of the Peace Neville. At this point, Neville was undoubtedly smacking his chops at the chance to deal out justice to the three who had managed to slip away the previous week.

This time the county was prepared with a volley of seven credible witnesses, and the defendants were bound over for trial in the First District Court. Unable to make bail, they cooled their heels in jail for more than two weeks until the First District Court was scheduled to convene its term.

It was at the Rich County Jail that Lant made his first of many escape attempts. Using a heavy iron bar torn from the door of the cell, Lant and his cellmates were busy trying to pry the bars from the window when the curious jailer came to investigate the source of all the noise. Given five more minutes, the three would have successfully flown the coop.

But that wasn't the worst of it for David Lant: his alias was blown. The jailer, a deputy sheriff from Vernal, recognized him as the young drunkard who had been shot in the Exchange Saloon. It was still a comedy of errors, though: while the local paper reported him as hailing from Payson, it still reported his last name as Lance.

On the morning of September 7, 1897, the three outlaws were led into the courtroom of thirty-one-year-old judge Charles Hart. In

David Lant was incarcerated at Utah State Penitentiary on September 8, 1897, to serve an eight-year sentence for theft. He escaped on October 8 after serving only thirty days.

the audience was Henry Sellon, who had been subpoenaed from Fort Bridger to testify against the men who had concealed their booty in his wagon. As charges were read, all three pleaded guilty to burglary. Hart then pronounced what today seems like a harsh sentence for stealing a suit of clothes: Ferguson was given a term of four years in the Utah State Penitentiary. Johnson and Lant (still under the alias of David Jones) were each sentenced to *eight years* at the penitentiary.

The following day, David Lant—just six days shy of his twenty-third birthday—was escorted through the gates and handed over to officials at the Utah State Penitentiary. Like every other prisoner before him, he was interviewed; he listed his occupation as "farmer" and his religion as "Mormon." He could read and write and was unmarried. And also like every other prisoner before him, he was examined for marks—he had the bullet scars from his fight at the saloon, a bevy of other scars, and badly decayed teeth—given a haircut, outfitted with a striped prison uniform, and made to sit for a mug shot. He was assigned the number 952.

Once they mingled with the general prison population, it appears that the three permanently went their separate ways. But David Lant lost no time mourning the loss of his old friends: within just a few days he teamed up with inmate 939, twenty-two-year-old Harry Tracy, regarded by Butch Cassidy's biographer as "the most desperate outlaw who ever entered Brown's Hole—the John Dillinger of his time."[66] Harry later became known as "Mad Dog" Tracy, a moniker that fit his disposition well. The two would become notorious across three states within an astonishingly brief time.

Interestingly, Harry was also in prison for stealing a suit of clothes, a crime to which he had also pleaded guilty. He had broken into a home in Provo, stolen the clothes, gotten arrested, failed to post bail, and been sentenced to a year for his crime by the Fourth District Court in Provo. (Apparently they were much more lenient in the big city.) Born Harry Severns in Wisconsin, he had spent his early and evidently criminal-free years as a logger, then left home in his teens to wander through the northern states, spending time in Montana and Washington—a time during which he adopted the alias Harry Tracy. He had eventually turned up in an abandoned house near the railroad depot in Provo where he was camping with four other railroad hoboes.

Harry was shorter and leaner than David; could also read and write; was also unmarried; also had badly decayed and broken teeth; and listed his occupation as cook (possibly a trade he learned in the logging camps where he worked as a teen). With deep-set dark eyes, he was often described as "swarthy" and was several times listed as a "mulatto" on sheriff bulletins. He had been in prison since July 11 that year, a few months longer than David.

And he didn't intend to stay.

Though his term was only a year— much shorter than Lant's—he had already started forming plans to escape. Those plans included two accomplices: twenty-four-year-old W. H. Brown, a heavily tattooed inmate serving a three-year sentence for robbery, and twenty-one-year-old Frank Edwards, serving a ten-year sentence for burglary, petty larceny, and housebreaking.

Oregon State Prison photo of Harry Tracy, David Lant's partner.

David Lant was eager and ready to join the other three in their escape plans.

When those plans were put into action, none of the three had been behind bars for long. Brown had been at the Utah State Penitentiary six months, Tracy three months, Lant only thirty days, and Edwards only twenty-one days when, on Friday, October 8, 1897, the four were part of a ten-convict work detail that was marched out the gate to work on a pipeline ditch intended to carry water from Parley's Canyon to the prison.

Work progressed smoothly and without incident all morning. At about two that afternoon, the warden arrived for an inspection tour at the construction site, about a mile from the prison, and exchanged pleasantries with guard John Van Steeter, who was keeping watch over the convicts. Within a few minutes the warden climbed back in his buggy and rode away to inspect other work-detail sites.

With the warden safely out of range, Tracy made his move. He dropped his shovel and almost simultaneously produced a .45-calibre revolver from the ditch. Shouting, he pointed the cocked revolver at the alarmed Van Steeter, who had no time to reach for his own weapon. His other three accomplices, including David Lant, stood guard while Tracy grabbed Van Steeter's weapon and ordered him to strip off his clothing. The other six work-detail convicts stood mutely by, assisting neither the guard nor the escaping inmates.

Within what seemed like seconds, Tracy had dumped his own clothes in the ditch, dressed in the prison guard's uniform, and led his three accomplices away from the work site and to the road that led away from the prison.

No one ever figured out who put the gun in the ditch.

Imagine the scene that unfolded next. The harried Van Steeter, dressed in a striped convict uniform, ran toward the prison waving his arms and shouting for help. At one point he ran into a nearby farmer's house and asked for a rifle; the farmer, of course, refused to give a rifle to a man dressed in prison stripes. The other six convicts, wanting to escape punishment, simply sat down in the dirt at the ditch site and waited.

In the meantime, Tracy, Lant, and their two accomplices reached the road and saw an older couple in a buggy on their way to buy chickens at a ranch in Parley's Canyon. Leveling his gun at the husband,

David Lant's partner, Harry Tracy, blamed the brutal work of breaking rock—similar to what's shown here—for his desire to escape from the Utah State Penitentiary.

Tracy commanded H. A. Stearns to stop the horse and get out of the buggy. While one convict held the horse and the other three forced Stearns to surrender his overcoat, Brown assured the wife that they didn't want to hurt anyone—that they were escaping because they had been mistreated.

Rummaging through the overcoat, Tracy kept the five dollars he found in the pocket but returned the pocket watch, saying they were "honest men" who would never steal a watch. As they climbed into the buggy and started off down the street, the wife cried out for her cherished lap robe, which the outlaws quickly threw out of the buggy.

About three hours later, the horse was discovered, ambling at a leisurely gait and pulling an empty buggy. The prisoners had gotten away.

The next morning's *Salt Lake Tribune* said the escape—one of the most daring in the history of the prison—was so quick and quiet that no one in the area even knew what had happened. A year and a half later in a Portland courtroom, Tracy justified his escape on the grounds that "they did not treat me right. I was breaking rock, and the large hammer they gave me to use hurt my hands, which were very tender.

I asked for a smaller hammer, and was refused." When he refused to work because his hands were bleeding and sore, he reported, prison officials "tied me up for five days, and I made up my mind to escape."[67]

The warden offered a fifty-dollar reward for each of the four escapees (close to a thousand dollars each in today's currency) and launched a three-man posse; the lawmen were able to follow the tracks of the prisoners into Parley's Canyon, where they lost the trail. Posses in several neighboring counties also took up the search, also to no avail.

The only information about the route of escape was later provided by David Lant, who detailed the adventure in a poem he wrote several months later. Apparently he and Tracy made their way to Park City and stopped to rest for a few days in a heavily forested area of Summit County. They had been supplied provisions by an unidentified source, and, smiling, watched from their vantage point as the posses tried to track them.

From the timbered area around Park City, they made their way to Vernal, where they were aided and abetted by local residents convinced that the two were just good Mormon boys temporarily sowing their wild oats. Uintah County Sheriff William Preece, himself a Mormon, launched a desperate search of his own when he learned the suspects were in his territory—and came under condemnation by the locals for raiding three houses during his search.

An editorial in the *Vernal Express* pretty much summed up the attitude of the locals when it said there was "a class of people in this valley that will shield any criminal that comes along and it makes it hard for an officer to do anything." The editorial further said that those who shielded the outlaws should be "given a term in the pen or a heavy fine for their pains."[68]

Lant and Tracy continued to be pursued. On November 15—more than a month after their daring escape—they were blamed for the theft of six horses from a schoolhouse at Fort Duschesne, Utah. When they drove the horses to an Indian camp and traded one of the horses for four Navajo blankets, Preece offered rewards to the Indians if *they* could capture the pair.

The two were finally spotted near Duchesne with another ex-convict, Robert Atwood, who had served a one-year term in the Utah State Penitentiary for grand larceny. Preece and his posse gave chase.

Lant, Tracy, and William Bascom—a legitimately good Mormon boy who liked to hang around with the outlaws—were engaged in a rope-trick game near a large chicken coop outside Duchesne when they saw in the distance four men on horses, galloping hard toward them. Harry Tracy asked for David Lant's spyglass, propped it on the chicken coop, and brought the horsemen into focus.

"It's the law," he growled. Then, reaching for his rifle, he assured the others, "I'll take care of this."

William Bascom asked him to wait while he tried to identify the approaching riders. "Wait!" he cried. "Those men are my family!"

Sure enough, Preece had deputized three of his Mormon relatives—John W. B. Bascom, Wal Lybbert, and David Manwaring—and the four were closing in fast on Lant and Tracy. Not wanting a showdown, the law-abiding and God-fearing Will Bascom gave the pair of outlaws his horse and told them to get out as fast as they could.

The four-man posse followed the trail of the outlaws to the Atwood ranch house at the spot where Branch Creek and Lybbert Gulch came together. Barging through the front door, they saw only Mrs. Elizabeth Atwood, rocking peacefully atop her braided rag rug. When questioned, she denied having seen any of the men and went back to her needlework.

Preece and his posse—determined to get their men—went out the back side of the house and followed the horse's tracks along the creek until they disappeared. When the four barged back into the house, imagine their frustration: Mrs. Atwood was leaning against the wall. The rocker had been shoved aside. The rag rug was bunched up to reveal a trap door to an empty cellar, where the outlaws had been hiding.

When questioned why she had harbored the fugitives, Mrs. Atwood, a Mormon herself, simply shrugged her shoulders. Her son Charlie—who would later serve a term at the penitentiary for grand larceny—was friends with the two boys, she reported. They liked to have fun together. And that's not all: They were all just wayward Mormon boys who were waiting for a chance to repent, she said. She hoped her shelter and protection would convince them to go straight.

After a few more failed attempts to catch up with Lant and Tracy, Sheriff Preece decided they had left the country, and he stopped his dogged efforts to capture them. But nothing could be farther from the truth: The two had met up with a few other outlaws and were cooling their heels at a camp outside Vernal. There they were discovered by Deputy Marshall Perry Young, who was traveling through the area on totally unrelated business. Stumbling on the surprised outlaws, Young recognized one of the men who was pointing a rifle at him as David Lant, who had been sentenced to—and escaped from—the Utah State Penitentiary. Calmly explaining his business, Young was allowed to go away unharmed.

As soon as Young returned to Vernal, of course, he alerted Sheriff Preece, who immediately formed another posse and took off in pursuit of Lant and Tracy. Arriving at the camp, he found nothing more than the dying embers of a campfire and hints of an abandoned camp.

The close encounter was the final straw for Lant and Tracy. They decided not to risk another close call and headed for the Hole-in-the-Wall. By then, though, most outlaws had abandoned the Hole in favor of an area to the south known as Powder Springs, and Lant and Tracy followed suit—just in time to be drawn into a tragic confrontation between the law and the outlaws.

It all started on the ranch near Powder Springs owned by Valentine S. Hoy, nestled along Red Creek just over the Wyoming border and a few miles from the Colorado line. Hoy's wife, Julia, was in Chicago recovering from surgery performed there; she planned to return sometime the middle of March. Hoy's two children were staying with family friends in Rock Springs.

The ground floor of the ranch house was occupied by five cowboys who had randomly roomed there over the winter. All but one had participated in at least some criminal activity, including murder; the only "clean" tenant was fifteen-year-old William Strang, whose parents lived in Vernal.

On the night of February 16, 1898, the five sat around a poker table, drinking, gambling, and roughhousing. The game wore on until the threadbare hours of the morning, around four o'clock. Three hours later, the bleary cowboys, exhausted from the marathon the night before, gathered around the table for breakfast. Still in a roguish mood, fifteen-year-old Strang pulled the chair out from under outlaw Pat Johnson, who fell to the floor. Laughing, Strang bolted from the house. Johnson, not in a mood for messing around, leaped to his feet and ran after the boy.

Grabbing his pistol, he stepped outside the door and fired in Strang's direction. Though later insisting he meant only to frighten the boy, Johnson hit his target—the bullet penetrated Strang's abdomen and lodged near his spine, throwing him to the frozen ground.

Strang was immediately carried into the house and attended to, and one of the cowboys raced to Rock Springs to summon a doctor. Despite everyone's best efforts, the boy died nineteen hours after being shot. Johnson, an Australian immigrant rumored to have murdered a man in Utah six years earlier, didn't see what all the fuss was about. He returned to the table, ate his breakfast, and then took off about three hours after the shooting. While one of the cowboys remained at the ranch nursing the boy until he died, he too took off, as did the other three cowhands. Even if Johnson hadn't intended to kill the boy, they reasoned, they all had enough blemishes on their records that none wanted to answer to the law.

Hoy himself was on his range searching for rustled cattle when news of the killing reached him. He immediately returned to the house, along with a number of concerned neighbors. Because the snows were too deep to take the boy's body to his parents' home in Vernal, he was buried in the frozen ground at the Red Creek ranch.

Subsequent investigations started to cast doubt on the story that the death was unintended, and the residents of nearby Brown's Hole were whipped into a frenzy over what they saw as the senseless slaughter of a mere boy. While they had traditionally fraternized with and even protected the outlaws who frequented the Hole, they now became suspicious and were quick to accuse if they suspected any violation. Especially unwelcome were outlaws who were "bad"—criminals who didn't mind being tough, including David Lant and Harry Tracy. In fact, most of the residents of the Hole had taken to packing firearms as a precaution.

Completely unaware of the killing at the Red Creek ranch, a pair of Colorado lawmen started out for Utah to try to recover some rustled cattle and stolen horses, armed with warrants for the arrest of the perpetrators. The snow was so deep that they had to travel by sled part of the way. As they traveled, they continued to catch glimpses of three armed horseback riders leading two pack horses on the trail ahead. The three unknown riders eventually left the road and headed across the high bluffs toward Douglas Mountain, arousing suspicion of the lawmen.

Exhausted, the Colorado lawmen finally reached Brown's Hole, where they lodged overnight on the Bassett ranch—and learned for the first time of William Strang's murder. They were startled to learn that the man accused of the murder was Pat Johnson—one of the men for whom they had a warrant. Their thoughts returned to the three horsemen they had followed earlier that day. They asked Bassett if he could round up a posse of Hole residents who would be willing to chase the three unknown horsemen; they would start out at daybreak the next morning.

At daybreak, nine men—including rancher Valentine Hoy—started in relentless pursuit of the three riders, one of whom they believed could be William Strang's killer. They were right on the money. Pat Johnson *was* one of the three riders. The other two were David Lant and Harry Tracy.

The posse followed the trail all day and suddenly came upon the riders' campsite. The three outlaws were gone but had obviously been taken by surprise. They got away with only their weapons and the clothes on their backs. All their other gear—bedding, provisions, food, and all five horses—was still at the campsite.

Trying to find the outlaws was foolhardy: the sheer cliffs and steep, rugged slopes of Douglas Mountain were home to countless recesses and caves. It would be almost impossible to find them—but the wisest strategy was to wait them out. The outlaws had to either stay in the mountains, where they would freeze to death, or come out and attempt an escape on foot, making them an easy target. The lawmen gathered up all the provisions and took the five horses back to Bassett's ranch as the freezing nighttime temperatures descended.

Lant, Tracy, and Johnson at first scrambled toward Brown's Hole on the ice of the Green River. But when the powerful currents of the Green River tumbled out from under the ice and plummeted over the rocks into Lodore Canyon at the entrance of Brown's Hole, the exhausted outlaws had no choice but to retrace their steps. They made the decision to return to the camp and ambush the posse when it returned.

When seven members of the posse arrived at the campground the next morning, two lawmen stayed with the horses at the camp while the other five inched their way up the rocky slope in pursuit of the outlaws. The terrain was so rugged that they progressed mere inches at a time, clutching at rocks and shrubbery.

By midafternoon they came to a huge boulder with a fissure just wide enough for one man at a time to pass through. On their side of the boulder were the dying embers of a fire the outlaws had used to warm themselves; beyond the fire, their tracks were scattered.

Valentine Hoy, disregarding the warning of the others, stepped toward the opening in the huge boulder. Two rifles blasts in quick succession ripped through the air; Hoy dropped to his knees, dying almost instantly from a bullet through his heart. It was later learned that Tracy fired the single shot that killed Hoy from a distance of only six feet away; the second shot was a reflex action of Hoy's finger on his own rifle.

Tracy appeared through the fissure, reaching for Hoy's weapon; a lawman yards behind Hoy fired a shot that didn't hit Tracy but sent him retreating without getting the gun.

For more than an hour, the outlaws stayed on the other side of the boulder, and the lawmen took shelter behind rocks and shrubs. The silence was deafening, and nerves were raw. At one point Tracy appeared at the fissure again but disappeared when a sheriff raised his rifle to his shoulder.

It was a true standoff, and the outlaws had the advantage as far as a vantage point was concerned. But time and the elements favored the posse: the outlaws had nowhere to go without getting progressively weaker and freezing to death. The sheriff's priority became getting his posse safely off the mountain. He whispered his command. One by one, each lawman backed slowly down the washout while the others kept their weapons trained on the outlaws. Finally, all four were safely over the edge. They had no choice but to leave the lifeless Valentine Hoy on his knees, leaning against the edge of the fissure.

Returning to the camp, they found only one of the two posse members waiting for them. And that's when things got interesting.

The two had earlier seen a lone horseman climb to the top of a high hill and discharge his rifle three times in the air. After an interval—as though expecting an answer but receiving none—he repeated the three shots.

His odd behavior aroused the suspicion of the two guards, who mounted their horses and took a small detour so it would appear they had come upon him accidentally. One of the posse—Eb Bassett, whose father owned Bassett's ranch—recognized the lone horseman as John Bennett, a close friend of Pat Johnson's who had been at the scene when William Strang was killed. Bennett had a long criminal history that included charges of forgery, burglary, assault, and attempted rape, among others. According to one Brown's Hole resident, he had at one time or other threatened to kill nearly every man in the valley.

The two posse members engaged Bennett in an easy conversation, claiming they were looking for some stray stock. Bassett then suggested that Bennett come with him to the ranch, where he could eat and rest protected from the weather. Since he was acquainted with the Bassetts, Bennett accepted the invitation without thinking twice. The other posse member said he'd keep looking for the stray stock—and as soon as Bassett and Bennett were out of sight, he scrambled back to the camp to meet the rest of the posse.

Because Bennett's horse was exhausted, he and Bassett traveled slowly to Brown's Hole. The posse, on the other hand, used shortcuts to pound into the ranch just a short time ahead of the other two. Bassett went to stable the horses while Bennett ambled into the ranch house. In the kitchen was Josephine Bassett MacKnight and her two young children; she was making cookies. Bennett leaned his gun against the doorway, as was customary when entering a residence, and greeted Josie, who offered him some cookies.

While the famished Bennett sat at the table and began wolfing down the warm cookies, posse member Ethan Farnham—unknown to Bennett—casually walked through the door, stepped up to the washbasin, washed his hands, and then approached Bennett like an old friend. Bennett put down his cookie. The rest of the posse stayed hidden just outside the door. Josie froze in fear, her back to the outlaw at the table.

Farnham smiled and asked if the man was John Bennett. When Bennett nodded, Farnham asked him to stand up, saying he had some papers he wanted to read to him. Producing the arrest warrant, Farnham ordered Bennett to put his hands in the air. His gun still leaning against the doorway, Bennett was cuffed without incident and taken next door to the Lodore post office, which was used as a temporary jail. There he was cuffed to a cot and guarded by Farnham.

In the meantime, Lant, Tracy, and Johnson remained on the run without horses or provisions in the rugged snow-covered country outside Brown's Hole. Taking Hoy's rifle with them, the three decided to head back to Powder Springs, where they figured they could somehow get some horses and provisions.

Early the next morning, March 2, 1898, several posses departed from Bassett's ranch. Several went in search of the outlaws, while another went to retrieve the body of Valentine Hoy. His wife had received a telegram reporting his death and was on her way home from Chicago to arrange for his funeral.

Just before noon—a point at which most of the ranch was deserted—seven or eight masked men rode into the yard, dismounted, and made their way into the post office building, where John Bennett remained cuffed to the cot and a weary Ethan Farnham still kept his guard. The masked men hadn't been too picky about their disguises: one sported a woman's black stocking over his head, while another had secured a pair of pink women's underwear around his face with a piece of clothesline. Two pointed muskets at the startled Farnham, shackled him, and instructed him to keep quiet. The others released Bennett from the cot, cuffed his wrists behind his back, pulled a burlap bag over his head, and led him outside to the corral gate.

With two vigilantes still guarding Farnham in the post office building, the others fashioned a noose, threw the rope over the crosspiece of the corral gate, and slipped the noose around Bennett's neck. Pleading for mercy and promising to tell all he knew, Bennett vehemently denied aiding the outlaws. His pleas fell on deaf ears. The men tightened the noose and hoisted a wailing Bennett into the air.

Leaving Bennett's body swinging lifeless from the corral gate, the men removed their disguises, strolled into the ranch house, washed their hands, and sat at the table for dinner. All were residents of Brown's Hole.

That afternoon, Deputy Sheriff Farnham cut Bennett's body down, wrapped it in a Navajo blanket, and buried it several yards from the ranch house. By the time a sheriff rode into the Hole with a warrant for Bennett's arrest on a charge of burglary, the deed was done.

By Friday, March 4, an unprecedented posse of approximately sixty lawmen from Utah, Wyoming, and Colorado were combing the hills in search of David Lant, Harry Tracy, and Pat Johnson. There were occasional evidences of the three, including a smoldering campfire where, desperate for food, they had butchered and eaten a young colt.

Deep snow, howling winds, and numerous narrow gulches impeded the progress of the posse, whose members grew increasingly more frustrated as the hours wore on. Added to their considerable frustration was fear that the outlaws would ambush them and fight to the death, killing one or more of their number.

By midafternoon, five of the lawmen finally spotted three men on foot about six miles from Powder Springs and a few miles from the Wyoming border. Commanded to halt, the three men instead began to run. The lawmen began firing rounds into the snow all around the outlaws as a strategy to obscure their vision. Pat Johnson turned, raised his hands, and walked toward the lawmen; Farnham apprehended and cuffed him. David Lant and Harry Tracy kept running and dived into a snow-filled gulch but did not return fire.

Determined to put an end to the manhunt, the lawmen surrounded the gulch, hid as best they could behind rocks and shrubs, and shouted for the desperate pair to surrender. Lant stayed silent; Tracy hurled profane defiance into the bitter wind.

For what seemed like hours, the standoff continued. Each demand for surrender was answered with Tracy's profane cheekiness. Finally David Lant rose slowly, his hands in the air, and started to walk toward the lawmen. He knew his surrender meant a return to prison, but he must have preferred that to either freezing to death or being killed by one of the posse.

He was stopped dead in his tracks when Harry Tracy screamed, "Get back here, or I'll blow your head off!" Lant immediately plunged back into the gulch.

The standoff continued.

Finally, Tracy demanded to know if the posse was comprised of lawmen. He would give up, he said—but not to a bunch of sheepherders and cowhands who would simply murder him on the spot. Assured that the five were indeed lawmen, David Lant stumbled out of his hiding place on frozen feet, his hands high above his head. A few steps behind Lant staggered Harry Tracy. Both were cuffed, and lawmen confiscated their weapons—including Winchester rifles (one of which had belonged to Valentine Hoy), revolvers, and David Lant's lariat rope.

It had been only three days since Valentine Hoy had been murdered on Douglas Mountain, but all three outlaws were in grim physical condition, battered by the cold. With only a single meal of horsemeat to sustain them through three days, the outlaws had covered nearly forty miles of brutal territory on foot through deep snows and bitter winds. Their clothes were torn and filthy; their boots were split at the seams; and their feet were bloody and nearly frozen. They had wrapped pieces of the colt's hide around their feet in an attempt to protect them from the elements.

Lant and Johnson were silent during the ride to the Jack Edwards sheep camp—the destination the outlaws were seeking in the hope of finding food and fresh horses—but Tracy kept up an almost ceaseless banter. At one point he told the officers, "Give me a cup of coffee, a fresh horse, and twenty-five yards head start and I won't bother you no more." It was an offer *all* the lawmen could easily refuse.

After spending the night at the sheep camp, the posse and its prisoners made its way back to Brown's Hole, where lawmen had a challenge to subdue a vigilante spirit. It seems Brown's Hole residents wanted three more graves lined up next to that of John Bennett—and only a tough old woman with a mean mouth and a loaded rifle was able to keep the peace.

Instead of a lynching, a preliminary hearing was held at the Bassett ranch house by Justice of the Peace James S. Hoy—the brother of Valentine Hoy, whose frozen body was being carried in the bed of a wagon to his home in Rock Springs. Posse members and neighbors alike crammed into the ten-room ranch house to hear the charges against Pat Johnson, Harry Tracy, and David Lant. Johnson and Lant were solemnly quiet; Tracy was arrogant and belligerent as he heard the charges against him in the cold-blooded murder of Valentine Hoy. In the end, Johnson was bound over to Wyoming officials to stand trial in the murder of young William Strang; Tracy and Lant were ordered held without bail to stand trial before the Ninth District Court at Hahns Peak, Colorado, for the murder of Valentine Hoy.

It's a miracle total bedlam was avoided. All three prisoners were placed under double guard in the post-office-turned-jail. As an additional protective measure, more than sixty men unofficially kept guard outside the jail, stalking the building like a band of coyotes and being warmed by the blaze of a roaring bonfire. Occasionally talk of a lynching took place—and each time, Sheriff William Preece simply walked away, giving his tacit approval. After all, these were Utah men; they had no vested interest in helping either Colorado or Wyoming lawmen have their day in court.

The Colorado and Wyoming lawmen *did* have a vested interest, though, and were determined to get their men to court in one piece. They spent a sleepless night roaming around the edges of the campfire, subduing the talk of lynching and encouraging the men to let justice prevail. Numbers were squarely on the side of the vigilantes, and the only thing that prevented them from taking the law into their own hands was the lack of a leader who was willing to take the first step.

The next morning—Sunday, March 6—Wyoming officials started the long ride to Rock Springs with Pat Johnson shackled to the cinch ring of the saddle in which he was mounted. At the same time, Colorado officials accompanied the shackled David Lant and Harry Tracy, tied in the bed of the sheriff's wagon, on the even longer ride to Hahns Peak. Both groups took untraveled roads to reach their destinations, hoping to avoid an almost certain lynching.

In the meantime, the Utah members of the posse returned to Vernal, where jubilant residents burned David Lant and Pat Johnson in effigy.

By the next day, Pat Johnson was behind bars in the Rock Springs city jail. Within a few hours he was joined by Charles Teeters, one of the poker players rumored to have participated in the shooting of William Strang. Worried that local citizens in Hoy's hometown might take vigilante action in the highly emotional atmosphere, the sheriff secretly moved the prisoners in the dark of the night fourteen miles to the county jail at Green River. Both pleaded not guilty to the murder of Strang; Teeters was eventually exonerated but Johnson received a life sentence for the killing.

Meanwhile, David Lant and Harry Tracy finally arrived in Hahns Peak after being interviewed by the press in both Craig and Steamboat Springs. Journalists in both towns remarked that while Harry Tracy was sullen and vicious, David Lant was cool, uncommunicative, and did not look like a criminal. On Thursday, March 10—six days after their capture in the snowy gulch—Lant and Tracy were finally incarcerated in the Routt County Jail at Hahns Peak, Colorado.

Immediately, Utah Governor Heber M. Wells wired Colorado officials, asking for the return of Lant and Tracy to Utah; after all, they had escaped from the Utah State Penitentiary, and he wanted them to finish their term there. Colorado Governor Alva Adams, knowing nothing about the murder of Valentine Hoy, readily agreed to return the prisoners to Utah. Colorado would get in its licks, he said, after the prisoners had finished serving their time in Utah.

Utah governor Heber M. Wells sought extradition of David Lant.

Two days later, with Utah officials en route to collect their prisoners, Governor Adams did an about-face: He had learned the details of the Hoy murder and now refused to surrender his prisoners to Utah lawmen. He wanted time to assess the probability of convicting the two on Hoy's murder before he agreed to give the prisoners up. After all, they were both serving time for mere burglaries in Utah. He had the chance of sewing up a murder rap in Colorado, and he wanted to make sure his chances of that were good.

Meanwhile, back at the ranch, David Lant and Harry Tracy were not simply sitting idly by in their jail cell while a pair of governors debated their status. Sheriff Charles Neiman ran a tight ship in his jail, and within a few days his two prisoners had the routine memorized. Just twelve days after being incarcerated, Lant pounced on the unwitting sheriff as he delivered the evening meal and beat him savagely with his fists until he lost consciousness.

Tracy wanted to kill the sheriff, but Lant persuaded him not to. They went through the sheriff's pockets, stealing a watch, ninety-four dollars in cash, and the keys to the jail. Tossing him on one of the bunks in their cell, they locked him inside and waited until all the lights were out in the sleepy town of Hahns Peak before bolting from the corridor. Running to the Whipple & Frazier barn, they stole two horses and rode bareback into the night. It was midnight before the bloodied Neiman was able to attract help, giving the outlaws a solid head start of two hours.

While drifting in and out of consciousness, Neiman had heard the outlaws discuss heading to the railroad at Wolcott, more than a hundred miles south and the nearest railway station to Hahns Peak. Resisting medical treatment, Neiman rounded up three volunteers and started toward Wolcott in nearly inhumane weather conditions, with temperatures dipping to twenty-five degrees below zero.

As it turns out, the posse was in much better condition than the two outlaws, who were dressed only in jail uniforms—they had no coats, no overshoes, and no gloves. It was easy for the posse to follow their fresh tracks in the snow, and soon they came upon the dying embers of a fire the two had set in an attempt to warm themselves. As they continued their pursuit through the night, they encountered long stretches where the outlaws had obviously walked, leading the horses and trying to keep their blood circulating in the freezing conditions.

A few miles outside Steamboat Springs, the posse discovered the site of a second fire—in an abandoned cabin owned by a local resident. Galloping into Steamboat Springs a little after 5 A.M., the bloodied and battered Sheriff Neiman gathered up a group of men willing to assist in the chase. Several posses were organized and headed in every direction out of town, though Neiman remained convinced that the outlaws were headed for Wolcott, still more than eighty-five miles away. Neiman and a Steamboat Springs volunteer boarded a stagecoach sleigh being used to travel the heavily snow-packed road between Hahns Peak and Wolcott, hoping to overtake the outlaws before they reached the rail station.

The sleigh had gone only about seven miles south of Steamboat Springs when two men came running out of the W. J. Laramore ranch house, waving the stage in. As the stage slid to a stop, Neiman recognized the two: David Lant and Harry Tracy. It seems they had stopped at the ranch house, where they offered up a vague story about being cowboys on an emergency run and were treated to a warm breakfast. Learning of the stage, they had determined to ride it to Wolcott.

This time Neiman had the advantage: he and his volunteer shoved cocked revolvers at the outlaws. Unarmed and nearly frozen to the bone, the two offered no resistance. Laramore supplied Neiman with a fresh team and sleigh for the return trip to Hahns Peak while the stage driver continued south on his regular route to Wolcott.

When Neiman and his prisoners arrived in Steamboat Springs about ten that morning, his first stop was at the Adair Hardware Store, where he bought two heavy padlocks and a good length of log chain—which he none too gently fastened around each prisoner's neck. His next stop was the Sheridan Hotel, where he and his posse pounded down a hearty breakfast while his prisoners were guarded in the hotel office.

Just eighteen hours after making their break for freedom, Lant and Tracy were back behind bars in Hahns Peak. This time, Neiman took extra precautions against a jailbreak. Not only were the prisoners chained at the neck, but they were each outfitted with the Oregon Boot—a patented invention of Oregon State Penitentiary warden J. C. Gardner consisting of a twenty-five-pound iron leg shackle and an iron ankle brace that encircled the heel of the shoe. The Oregon Boot, which restricted wearers to steps of about eight inches, made walking difficult at best. Running was out of the question. (First introduced in 1866, the Oregon Boot was so barbaric that it was eventually used only for disciplinary measures.)

Lant and Tracy spent most of each day sleeping and most of each night yelling, screaming, profaning, and banging their Oregon Boots against the bars of their cells. Neiman had an agenda: he wanted to restore peace to the town, avoid a vigilante move by residents, and keep the two escape artists incarcerated until early September, when court would again convene at Hahns Peak. Using those arguments, he succeeded in moving his two prisoners to the Pitkin County Jail in Aspen, Colorado. They had spent a total of only twenty-nine days during two stays in Neiman's facility.

Upon arriving with their prisoners at the Pitkin County Jail in Aspen, Sheriff Charles Neiman and Deputy Sheriff Andy Underwood warned Sheriff Richmond Fisher that Lant and Tracy were seasoned escape artists who could spot even the most remote chance for breaking out. Securely positioned behind bars, Lant and Tracy were finally free of their neck chains and Oregon Boots. An article in the *Aspen Tribune* reassured residents of their safety: The jail, it boasted, was one of the most secure in the state and it would be next to impossible for the pair to escape.

David Lant, of course, did not share that opinion.

On Wednesday, June 22, 1898—seventy-four days after they had entered Pitkin County Jail and only halfway through their scheduled stay—Lant and Tracy replayed their escape from the Hahns Peak facility. As the jailer arrived to retrieve the dinner dishes, David Lant prevented him from latching the cell door and proceeded to beat him almost to death with an iron poker. The two then rushed into the jail office, found the jailer's revolver and keys, and returned to their cell.

The two led the semiconscious jailer to a bathtub where they washed the blood from his face and scalp (nice to get a wash, but stitches would later be required to close the gashes on the man's head). They then led him back to their cell, tied him to the bunk with a length of clothesline, and locked the cell door. Then they waited for the cloak of darkness before running from the jail.

About seven-thirty Sheriff Fisher returned to the courthouse. Alarmed when he couldn't find the jailer, he decided to inspect the cells. As he rounded a corner, he encountered Tracy, armed with the jailer's revolver. Fisher bolted from the corridor and ran upstairs to his office to grab his own revolver. Glancing out the window, he saw the two fugitives running across the railroad tracks toward the Roaring Fork River.

Fisher decided against chasing the outlaws himself. Instead, he sounded an alarm throughout Aspen and telegraphed nearby towns regarding the escape. While several groups found the outlaws' tracks in various places along the river, the two evaded capture.

Lant and Tracy were in desperate straits by then—they needed clothing, food, shelter, and money. Five days after their escape from Aspen, they donned masks and robbed a saloon in Breckenridge, Colorado, about fifty miles northeast of Aspen. They got away with $165 in silver (around a thousand dollars in today's currency) but were run out of the saloon by a gun-wielding bartender before they could penetrate the saloon's safe.

Their meager profit wasn't enough to sustain them for long. Less than a week later they burst into the Kokomo saloon, fifteen miles southwest of Breckinridge. This time they knew what they were doing, rushing in through both the front and rear door, disarming everyone in the saloon, and garnering $300 for their trouble. Leaving the saloon, they rushed into the nearby home of George W. Steve, treasurer of the local Odd Fellow's Lodge, where they beat his wife and got away with $460 of the lodge's funds.

Summit County Sheriff Jeremiah Detwiler and the town of Kokomo put up a combined reward of $250 (approaching five thousand dollars in today's currency) for capture of the two desperados, but it was to no avail. Within a week the two outlaws had pulled off three more successful robberies, getting away with $925 in cash and silver.

With that, they disappeared.

At the time of their disappearance, David Lant and Harry Tracy had known each other less than ten months since meeting for the first time behind bars in the Utah State Penitentiary. In those ten months, they had traveled hundreds of miles through three states, committed murder, kept lawmen on the run, escaped from a penitentiary, and broken free from two jails.

Harry Tracy reappeared two months later, continuing his life of crime. After murdering at least six or seven more men, the twenty-seven-year-old Harry Tracy took a bullet in the leg while being pursued by lawmen. Unable to stop the heavy bleeding from the wound, he refused to give the law the satisfaction of bringing him down. Dropping to the ground in a wheat field outside Creston, Washington, twenty-seven-year-old Harry Tracy pressed his revolver between his eyes and pulled the trigger. His suicide on the morning of August 6, 1902, ended his life of crime. He was buried at the Oregon State Penitentiary.

Not so with his former partner. At the ripe old age of twenty-three, David Lant simply evaporated after the robberies in Kokomo.

No one ever figured out what happened to him, where he went, or who he became.

Oh, the rumors were wild. Some said he was killed by Harry Tracy before the two separated. Others said he enlisted in the army and became a war hero in the Philippines. Still others claimed he was captured and ended up behind bars in a prison in the northwest. And some vowed he had tossed aside his outlaw ways and returned to Utah, where he became a respectable citizen using an alias.

None of the rumors was ever substantiated. And no one ever found evidence to support *any* continued existence of David Lant.

Not even his family knew what happened to him. While he randomly kept in touch with them during his early days as an outlaw, communications between them soon ceased. His brother John claims to have once brought David a change of clothes as he prepared to row a boat across Utah Lake, west of Payson, after escaping from Colorado. Family legend claims that he occasionally secretly visited his elderly father, assuring him that he had never killed anyone. Again, no evidence exists to prove any of these claims.

Curiously, a "David Lant" of "Payson" signed the death certificate of the elder David T. Lant when he died in November 1908. Since no one else in the family was named *David*, descendants believe the reformed outlaw may have been at his father's side when the old man drew his final breath.

After being shot, shot at, nearly lynched, jailed three times, the subject of one of the most intense manhunts in the West, and part of one of the most notorious duos in outlaw history during his twenty-three short years, David Lant simply vanished.

CHAPTER SEVEN
Orrin Porter Rockwell

IF ANY MORMON OUTLAW COULD give Butch Cassidy a run for his money when it comes to fame and glory, it's Porter Rockwell. Authors, journalists, and government officials knew him as a scout, a gunman, a rough-and-tumble frontiersman, and a man with an iron nerve. His loyalty was legendary. Over a lifetime of adventure, Porter attracted the myth-makers, the curiosity-seekers, and the celebrity-chasers. In fact, at the time of his death, he was as well-known throughout the West as Brigham Young himself.

You probably already know a lot about Porter Rockwell—but there are some fascinating things about him you might *not* know. He was one of the first people to join the Mormon Church; at his death in the summer of 1878, he had been a member of the Church longer than anyone else then living. He was also one of the Church's most devoted members: After putting in a hard day of physical labor, he often picked berries or chopped wood late into the night, giving all his earnings to his boyhood friend Joseph Smith to pay for publishing the Book of Mormon.

While in Nauvoo he was ordained a Seventy, a position he held throughout the rest of his life. Joseph Smith prophesied that as long as Porter never cut his hair, his enemies would never harm him; that prophecy was fulfilled, despite one episode

Orrin Porter Rockwell, with his famed long hair and beard.

in which he gave all his hair to a woman who had lost hers. More about that later.

His loyalty to Joseph Smith, come thick or thin, was unswerving. Apparently that loyalty went both ways. During the hostilities in Missouri, Joseph Smith had this to say about his friend, Porter Rockwell: "He is an innocent and noble boy. May God Almighty deliver him from the hands of his pursuers. He was an innocent and a noble child and my soul loves him. Let this be recorded for ever and ever. Let the blessings of salvation and honor be his portion."[69]

He was a fiercely devoted bodyguard—first of Joseph Smith, then of Brigham Young, and finally of the territorial sheriff. At one point he *was* the sheriff.

He arrived in Utah with the first group of pioneers, boasting the nickname "the Destroying Angel." That's because nobody got away with much when Porter Rockwell was around. He is the only gunman to have killed more outlaws than Tom Horn, Bat Masterson, Doc Holladay, and Wyatt Earp combined—sometimes in his line of duty as a lawman, sometimes in self-defense. There is no indication at all that he ever killed out of revenge, anger, or passion; in fact, in many cases he exhibited extreme control.[70]

Asked once about his deadly accurate trigger finger, he told a crowd listening to United States vice-president Schuyler Colfax in 1869, "I never killed anyone . . . who didn't need killing." That would include Brigham Young's own nephew, who took Porter's bullet right through the heart for stealing a horse. But more about that later as well.

When President James Buchanan sent an army to Utah to quell a rumored rebellion against the United States, its progress was slow and painful. That's because Porter had been instructed to slow the army down without shedding any blood. To fulfill that charge, Porter crept among its camps each night under the cloak of darkness, silently tapping the pins out of its wagon wheels and scattering its horses across the prairie.

Porter was fiercely loyal and bold to jump to the defense of his fellow Mormons. He had his own kind of "special operations" when trying to fend off outsiders: "Use every exertion to stampede their animals and set fire to their trains. Burn the whole country before them, and on their flanks. Keep them from sleeping by night surprises;

blockade the road by felling trees or destroying the river fords where you can. Watch for opportunities to set fire to the grass before them that can be burned."[71] It was exactly the kind of mischief that gave Porter his fascinating dual identity. Sometimes he was the outlaw, and sometimes he was the law.

He was married to four women but was never a polygamist; his first wife divorced him, and the next two each died. He was persecuted for his Church membership, beaten nearly to death for his association with Joseph Smith, and thrown behind bars—kept in an unheated dungeon without any bedding for more than nine months—when accused of trying to kill a governor. More about that later, too. Through it all, he survived to become one of the most riveting figures of the Wild West.

Orrin Porter Rockwell was born June 28, 1813, in Belcher, Massachusetts, the oldest child of Orin and Sarah Rockwell. When Porter was only four, his father abandoned the family farm in Massachusetts—crops had no chance against the arctic temperatures the previous several winters—and hoped to get a new start in the small farming community of Palmyra, New York, then considered part of the frontier. Two years later, Joseph Smith Sr. bought the adjoining farm, relocating his family from Sharon, Vermont. Just like that, the Rockwells and the Smiths became next-door neighbors.

And they were close in ways other than proximity. Though Porter was almost eight years younger than Joseph Smith Jr., the two developed an unusually close bond because of a shared infirmity: a limp. Joseph Smith's was the result of an operation to remove a portion of diseased bone from his leg (you remember the story—he bravely subjected himself to the surgery without benefit of the numbing liquor). Porter Rockwell's was the result of a broken leg improperly set by a careless physician; for the rest of his life, one leg was two inches shorter than the other. *Two inches.* That's hardly insignificant. It was a lifelong source of embarrassment for Porter. Joseph often found himself defending his young friend from the taunts of bullies who ridiculed the way he walked. Later, the tables would be turned, and Porter was the one who defended Joseph.

Following the First Vision and visits from the angel Moroni, Joseph and his family often visited the Rockwell house and, by the flickering light of pine torches, shared incredible stories of the continent's ancient inhabitants. He may have been only ten at the time, but Porter listened intently and became one of Joseph's most ardent believers.

Porter and his mother were baptized members of the Church in June 1830, just two months after it was organized, making them some of the faith's first members. Porter was sixteen at the time. His father was baptized approximately two years later, and most of the rest of the family eventually followed suit.

When Joseph Smith moved the Church to Kirtland, Ohio, the Rockwell family sold their farm, traveled by barge on the Erie Canal, and traveled the last length of the journey by boat to Fairport, Ohio. After only a short time in Kirtland, the Rockwell family responded to a request by Joseph Smith to move to an area near Independence, Missouri, to establish a second gathering place for the Church. Orin Rockwell and his family were with the first group of Mormons to settle in Missouri.

Porter worked hard to help his father establish the new farm but also acquired a farm in his own name that he worked tirelessly to develop. His independence, capacity, and diligent work ethic impressed Isaac and Olive Beebe enough that they gave permission for their daughter to marry the industrious young man. The wedding of Orrin Porter Rockwell and Luana Beebe on February 2, 1832, was the first Mormon wedding in Jackson County, Missouri, and was celebrated by all the Mormon settlers in the area.

Porter now had a bride to support, and he came up with the perfect solution: he established a ferry that crossed the Big Blue River near Independence. His enterprise was an immediate hit—after all, there was an enormous influx of Mormon settlers streaming into the area, and they all needed to get across the river at some point. Porter then flexed his muscles and constructed a home near the ferry; with its ideal location, it was often used for Church meetings. In fact, a conference to commemorate the third anniversary of the founding of the Church was held April 6, 1833, at Porter's Ferry, as the location came to be known.

All things pointed to a happily-ever-after for the young couple.

But that was before the mobs.

Mob violence was driven home to Porter Rockwell on July 20, 1833, when an armed mob—its members painted to look like Indians—clambered aboard the ferry and demanded to be shuttled to the Mormon side of the river. Neither Porter nor his father was armed, and both were helpless against the coarse mob and its threats of depravities against Mormon women and children. Porter made up his mind then and there that he would never be caught unprepared again.

A little more than three months later a mob approached Orin Rockwell's property; Sarah sent her husband and sons into the woods to hide, knowing they would be killed if the mobs found them. Holding Sarah and her young daughters at knifepoint, the infuriated mob completely destroyed their home and vowed they would be back—this time to kill the men.

Porter was outraged when he heard of the attack.

But things became very personal just a short time later when he returned from the ferry to find Luana sobbing next to the ruins of their home. A mob had torn off the roof, ripped apart the timbers, and pulled down every log in the cabin. It was an attack that changed the course of Porter's life: He vowed he would never again be unarmed.

Porter was as good as his word. He never again went for so much as a casual stroll around the neighborhood without carrying a gun.

Porter dug in his heels and maintained that no one could drive him and his family out of Jackson County. But when mob violence became too much to tolerate, Church leaders signed a pledge that the Mormons would leave Jackson County by January 1, 1834. That meant *all* the Mormons. Including Porter Rockwell. He and his family made their way across the river into Clay County with only the things they could carry in their arms.

That wasn't the end of it—for Porter or for the rest of the Mormons. Within a few years they were driven out of Clay County, too; Porter, Luana, and their two young daughters set up housekeeping in Far West, Missouri. By the time Joseph Smith arrived a year later, Far West had grown into a bustling community of more than five thousand, boasting hundreds of buildings, more than two thousand farms, a public square, and a temple site.[72] Expelled from other settlements, Mormons were starting to spread outside the boundaries of Caldwell County—there simply wasn't room enough to accommodate them all.

Their growing numbers worried their non-Mormon neighbors. Pretty soon Caldwell County natives were reacting to the same issues that had so inflamed the citizens of Jackson County and Clay County.

They were bothered by religious differences, but it didn't stop there. They also feared the political power of such a large group of people, especially considering the Mormons' opposition to slavery and their more accommodating stance toward the Indians.

As for Joseph Smith, he faced a more pressing personal problem: Those he had counted on to help him build the Church were falling away at a rapid clip. Some of his most loyal supporters became his loudest and most verbal detractors once they got to Missouri. In response, Sidney Rigdon, a member of the First Presidency, demanded in writing that any dissenters leave the county immediately. Hyrum Smith signed his support. So did Porter Rockwell; because he couldn't write his name, he signed with an *X*. His was the sixty-ninth of the eighty-three signatures on the document.[73]

Each of the eighty-three who put pen to paper on that occasion had his own reasons for doing it. Porter's was simple. He was then, and continued to be, steadfastly loyal to his boyhood friend Joseph Smith.

That unswerving loyalty informed many of Porter's subsequent actions. He was one of the first to join the Danites ("Sons of Dan"), a secret militia group formed to root out any traitors among the ranks, though he played a minor role in the organization and never held

The interior of Liberty Jail; Porter Rockwell smuggled two augers to Joseph Smith while the Prophet was being held prisoner in an attempt to help him escape from the jail.

any leadership position. And in the ensuing Missouri War, Porter was defending the outer borders of Far West as he watched Joseph Smith surrender, get arrested, and get hauled off to Liberty Jail.

With Joseph in Liberty Jail, Porter again put his *X* to a document pledging his loyalty to the Church and its leader. The last groups of Mormons were beating a path out of Missouri and settling in the new "city beautiful," Nauvoo—but some were too destitute to make the trip after all the persecution and violence. Porter was one of a handful of men who signed a document pledging to sell all they had to help the poor leave Missouri.[74] That's not all: Porter and the others pledged to stay behind until all the Mormons were out of Missouri, just in case they encountered any more problems from the locals. With Porter committed to staying behind, his wife and children made the trip to Nauvoo without him.

While Joseph Smith was behind bars, Porter became his messenger, helping Joseph stay in touch with various people on the outside—mostly Brigham Young. He brought food and drink to the prisoners as well.

That's not all: Liberty was the site of Porter's first attempted jailbreak, even though he wasn't the one behind bars.

The prisoners had tried to flee once before, Joseph told Porter, by charging through the cell door when it was opened to accommodate a visitor. But a pair of alert guards had slammed the door shut in their faces, ending all hope of escape. Driven to the edge of desperation by the primitive conditions in the jail, Joseph and his fellow prisoners were more determined than ever to get some distance between them and their captors. And they knew just the person to help.

For his part, Porter came up with what seemed to be a foolproof plan. On his next visit he smuggled two augers into the jail, recommending that the prisoners bore a hole through the wall. It was brilliant. Joseph and the others had plenty of time on their hands, and they enthusiastically started drilling. Even though the hard rock walls of the jail were four feet thick, they kept drilling. The inmates were within a few inches of freedom when the augers simply gave out.

Joseph hit up Porter again, asking him to bring replacement handles for the augers. Porter willingly complied. But the long wooden handles were difficult to smuggle past the observant guards, and Porter was stopped in his tracks.

When it was all said and done, just one large rock—and less than a minute's scramble through the space—stood between the prisoners and freedom. According to Joseph, the sheriff didn't blame them for trying to escape. And Joseph was proud of his handiwork—"a fine breach that cost the county a round sum."[75] (They finally *did* escape while being transferred to another jail, but details are murky: it seems that the governor himself, tired of the embarrassment, orchestrated the escape. At the end, there were lots of guards in a drunken stupor on the floor of the judge's parlor, and one of the deputies actually supplied horses and invited Hyrum to gather up the other prisoners and take off.[76] No one had to ask him twice.)

With Nauvoo, the Mormons finally had a place to call their own—but leaders weren't going to take the years of persecution sitting down. On October 29, 1834, Joseph Smith and two other leaders set out for Washington, DC, where they planned to petition President Martin Van Buren and Congress for redress of the wrongs committed against them in Missouri. Part of the affidavit Joseph carried listed the property the Rockwell family had lost to the mobs in Missouri—valued at the stunning amount of nearly a quarter of a million dollars in today's currency. And sitting next to Joseph in the carriage was the man he had chosen to protect his life: Orrin Porter Rockwell, who left his wife just two days after their first son was born so he could protect the Prophet.

You know the rest. The Senate Judiciary Committee refused to help. The House of Representatives refused to help.[77] And President Van Buren, afraid of losing the Missouri vote in the next election, uttered his famous refusal: "Gentleman, your cause is just, but I can do nothing for you."

Fast-forward seven years and a handful of months. Luana was pregnant with their fourth child, and she'd just about had it. Life on the frontier was hard—even *without* relentless persecution. And don't even talk about having your house torn down around your shoulders. She thought Porter spent far too much time away from home—and now, expecting their fourth child, she demanded to be taken back to Independence so her aunt and uncle could help her with the birth.

Porter resisted. After all, there were warrants out for his arrest in Missouri because of his role in the Missouri War. Then there was that pesky extermination order signed by the governor, targeting the

Mormons (which, appallingly, was not rescinded until the late 1970s). And Porter had an especially prominent target on his back—the Missourians wanted him dead because he was so close to Joseph Smith.

For whatever reason, Porter finally relented. In February 1842, he took Luana—now eight months pregnant—to Independence. Helping his wife get settled, he used the alias James B. Brown and worked earning money by training horses for a local farmer. Their daughter was born on March 25, 1842, and was named Sarah after Porter's mother. Shrugging off threats to his personal safety, Porter remained with Luana in Missouri throughout her convalescence.

Porter may have hoped to save his struggling marriage by risking life and limb in Missouri on behalf of his wife, but it didn't work. Later that year Luana returned to Nauvoo, left her children to Porter's now-widowed mother, and divorced Porter. Her main complaint? He was more loyal to Joseph Smith than he was to her. She also accused him of being interested in polygamy—an unfounded claim, since he never practiced plural marriage.

As it turns out, the fact that Porter was in Missouri with Luana led to him being accused of the attempted assassination of Missouri governor Lilburn W. Boggs, the rascal who had signed the extermination order against the Mormons. (Just for the record, though, Boggs had lots of enemies other than the Mormons.)

Boggs had just finished dinner and had settled down in his parlor to read the newspaper on May 6, 1842. Two of his young daughters were with him; outside, the rain was pouring. Suddenly the explosion of a

Missouri governor Lilburn Boggs

single gunshot ripped through the air and a bullet smashed through the closed window. Boggs was hit four times by the single shot—twice in the back of the head and twice in the neck. The pistol was so overloaded with powder that the force of the shot sent it flying out of the assassin's hand; he ran from the scene before anyone could see him, leaving the gun where it landed in the mud a few yards from the house.

Boggs's oldest son ran for help, and soon the sheriff arrived with four doctors. Boggs was seriously injured, but recovered.

Investigation of the crime was sloppy at best. Not only that, stories seemed to change with the direction of the wind. A local merchant stepped forward, claiming the gun had been stolen from his store. At first he blamed a group of slaves who had been in the store. Later he changed his story, saying James B. Brown—remember Porter's alias?—had come in the store the same day, looking for that exact gun.

In the meantime, a five hundred-dollar reward was offered in the *Jeffersonian Republic* for a silversmith named Tompkins. Evidence against Tompkins was overwhelming, claimed the paper; lawmen were sure they had identified their man. The newspaper gave a blow-by-blow description of the man, one that bore no resemblance to Porter.

A week later, the same newspaper did an about-face, saying Tompkins was innocent. The real criminals, it reported, were Joseph Smith and Porter Rockwell. No matter that Joseph Smith was nowhere near Missouri—the paper claimed that a year earlier, Joseph Smith had prophesied that Boggs would die a violent death. It was simple, reported the paper: Joseph had sent Porter Rockwell to fulfill the prophecy.

In reality, such a prophecy was never uttered.

The crime was never solved, and Porter was never proven guilty. Porter himself scoffed off the accusation by saying, "I've never shot *at* anybody. If I shoot, they get shot. He's still alive, isn't he?" (In other words, *If I'd taken aim, he'd be dead.*) Joseph Smith made the same implication when he said, "It couldn't have been Porter—he'd have killed him."[78]

There were lots of logical reasons why Porter wasn't the assassin. In the first place, he had his own gun; why steal one? That's not all: if there was one thing Porter knew, it was guns. He knew better than to overload the gun with so much powder that it would buck out of his hand. Then there was his alibi: the day after the shooting, Porter was seen on a riverboat in St. Louis, and two weeks later he was back in Nauvoo—both journeys that would have been impossible to make that quickly from Independence.

No matter. A warrant was issued for the arrest of Porter Rockwell and Joseph Smith. A group of apostates in Nauvoo were only too happy to keep the rumors circulating.

In the meantime, Porter's wife showed up in Nauvoo with divorce papers, stating her intention to give her children to Porter's mother. Facing not only an arrest warrant but an antagonistic wife, Porter decided to get out of Dodge, as the saying goes.

Porter fled to the East and spent nearly a year on the lam but simply couldn't find work; the economy in that region was severely depressed. At one point, most people were working not for money but in exchange for food. Worried about Joseph's safety, Porter finally decided to return to Nauvoo by way of the Ohio River. It was a foolhardy decision. As he was nearing St. Louis, Elias Parker—a Mormon aboard the steamboat—recognized Porter from the "Wanted" posters tacked up and down the riverbank and turned him in so he could collect on the reward being offered.

Porter was arrested and hauled off to jail in St. Louis. Three days later, his ankles hobbled with irons, Porter was loaded onto a midnight stagecoach with eight other passengers, including the deputy to whom he was handcuffed. The February weather was particularly brutal, and the stage was not heated. Conditions were miserable.

But that was the least of the problem: The stagecoach driver appeared exceptionally fond of liquor, creating a white-knuckled ride for the passengers. On the second night, the driver slammed the coach into a tree, breaking the king bolt. While the terrified passengers shivered in the cold, Porter repaired the bolt and the coach was back on its way. A short time later, the inebriated driver rammed the coach into a ditch bank; working together, the passengers dislodged it. The driver was too impaired to continue, and despite the bad roads, the overloaded coach, and his leg irons, Porter managed to get the coach to the next stop.

After an intermittent stop in Jefferson City, where Porter was jailed for two days, he and his arresting officer finally arrived in Independence, where a crowd mobbed the stage and demanded that Porter be hanged at once. He was whisked away to jail for his own safety, and three days later appeared in court. Men armed with hickory clubs savagely beat Porter in the courtroom while younger boys kicked and punched him repeatedly.

Despite the false witness of the arresting officer, the magistrate was unable to charge Porter with a crime but still vowed to hold him for trial. Fearful the fomenting crowds would kill him, the magistrate confined Porter to prison.

Still hobbled with ankle irons, Porter was kept in an upper cell of the jail during the day and confined to a vermin-filled, unheated dungeon at night with only a pile of filthy straw on which to sleep. He existed on one meal a day—food he described as "not fit for dogs." The official charge was his alleged attempt on the life of Lilburn Boggs, but Porter knew there was more to it. Missouri officials were using him to ensnare Joseph Smith.

As a result, Porter tried another jailbreak. Having lost a significant amount of weight, he twice removed a stovepipe and gained access to the upper cell during the night, only to discover the cell door was locked.

Just as Porter was about to give up hope, he got a new cellmate—a man charged with fraudulent issue of US Treasury notes. The counterfeiter had been allowed to keep his saddlebags; tucked inside was a steel file. Porter heard opportunity knocking at the door and spent the next several days laboriously filing through his cuffs. Finally the two prisoners were ready to make their move.

The jailer arrived with supper. Porter had warned his cellmate not to eat too much of his succulent food because he'd be unable to run; ignoring Porter's advice, the man ate ravenously.

No sooner had the jailer entered the cell to collect the dishes than Porter leaped to his feet, shoving the jailer into the corner. The counterfeiter rushed through the open door, down the stairs, and out into the yard. As Porter ran through the door, he locked the jailer inside the cell, tossed the keys out a window and into the garden, bolted down the stairs, and made his dash for freedom.

Only one last obstacle stood between Porter and liberty: a twelve-foot outer wall. Summoning all his strength, he managed to scale it successfully and had dashed twenty yards toward the heavily wooded area on the other side when he heard the counterfeiter's cries for help. There had to be a split second when Porter weighed his options—but realizing that the counterfeiter's file had made escape possible in the first place, Porter went back up and over the wall and began boosting his cellmate over the top.

Once on the other side, he found his strength completely spent. The counterfeiter ran toward the woods but a group of vigilante neighbors caught him. Porter was no longer able to run; he walked back to the jail yard, where he was immediately threatened with hanging. The frenzied crowd pressed up the stairs behind the jailer, their threats echoing off the walls of the narrow stairway. After hesitating only a moment, the sheriff pushed Porter into the unlocked cell and invited the menacing crowd to have their way with him. Clutching his cellmate's saddlebag, he felt a four-pound bag of bullets inside and determined to use it to mash in the head of anyone who tried to put a rope around his neck.

During the next few minutes, Porter heard pistols cocking and saw nooses and bowie knives being passed among the crowd. But soon the room was cleared—and, having tried to escape only minutes earlier, Porter now locked himself in his cell for his own safety.

The jailer was not amused by Porter's escape attempt, and he determined to tighten security. Porter was tossed in the dungeon around the clock, his right hand cuffed to his left foot and his left hand cuffed to his right foot. Unable to sit up straight, he was in agony. The irons on his wrists were so tight they could barely lock. His food, were it possible, was even worse than before; if he refused to eat it, he got it again for his next meal until he finally gagged it down. Within three weeks he had become so thin that he could push the wrist irons up to his elbows.

Days turned to weeks, and weeks turned to months, and still Porter languished in the jail at Independence. And during the entire period of his nine-month incarceration, one thing was notably absent: Joseph Smith. The government's plot to lure Joseph to Missouri by holding Porter in prison hadn't worked. Officials decided it was time to try a more direct approach.

Imagine Porter's surprise when the sheriff strutted into his cell and thrust a heavy leather pouch at him. "It's just a down payment," the sheriff purred as Porter opened the pouch to discover it filled with gold coins—approximately $100,000 at today's value. "Get Joseph Smith to come to Missouri so we can arrest him, and you can name your price. We'll raise it. You can live a free and wealthy man among us. What do you think?"

Porter latched the pouch and shoved it back at the sheriff. "I will see you damned first," spat Porter.[79]

On another occasion, Porter overheard the jailer and a stranger, thinking Porter asleep, quietly discussing a plot against Joseph's life.

When Sarah Porter visited her son the next day, he sent her immediately back to Nauvoo to warn the Prophet of the threat.

Sarah Porter next turned her attention to raising funds in Nauvoo for her son's legal defense. Though he was personally penniless, Joseph Smith rallied—twice. First he went to the site of the temple construction, climbed on a large granite stone, and told the workers of Porter's predicament. When he passed his hat around, it came back full. Leaving the construction site, he happened upon a carnival and challenged a Goliath of a man to a wrestling match. Miraculously, Joseph defeated the much larger man. Between the prize money from the wrestling match and the generous donations at the temple site, Joseph had raised a hundred dollars for Porter's defense.

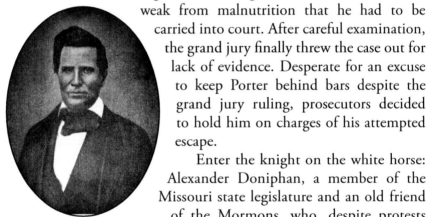

At the same time, Missouri finally convened a grand jury to investigate the case against Porter. Porter was so weak from malnutrition that he had to be carried into court. After careful examination, the grand jury finally threw the case out for lack of evidence. Desperate for an excuse to keep Porter behind bars despite the grand jury ruling, prosecutors decided to hold him on charges of his attempted escape.

Enter the knight on the white horse: Alexander Doniphan, a member of the Missouri state legislature and an old friend of the Mormons, who, despite protests that he was too busy to take the case, had been given the hundred dollars to defend

Attorney Alexander Doniphan

Porter. Doniphan immediately obtained a change of venue to Clay County, hoping for a better chance of acquittal.

Getting Porter to Clay County did little more than provide his captors with another chance at torture. He was pushed into a miserably poor saddle on a hard-trotting horse. His feet were tied under the horse and his hands were tied behind his back. He took off in the company of two officers and was soon joined by a stranger—later found to have frustrated the plans of a Missouri mob waiting to ambush him in the thick timber. Soon remanded back to Independence, the Clay County officers took Porter by a different route, again frustrating a mob intent on killing him.

Doniphan had his work cut out for him. It was true that Porter *had* tried to escape. There was no denying it. But Doniphan argued that it was a justified attempt—after all, Porter had been treated inhumanely and had been kept in prison for nine long months, far past his constitutionally guaranteed right to a fair and expedient trial. That's not all, pointed out Doniphan: Porter's "escape" attempt didn't meet the definition of the law, which required breaking a lock, a door, or a wall. Porter had "escaped" by exiting through an open door.

It was a solid argument, and the prosecution capitulated. Desperate for the last word, however, they sentenced Porter to a term of five minutes for the escape attempt. They still managed to keep him for an additional five hours while frantically but unsuccessfully trying to trump up some other charge against him. Finally, Doniphan walked Porter out of the jail at about 8 P.M. It was in direct fulfillment of a prophecy uttered by Joseph Smith on March 15, 1843, that Porter would "get away honorably from the Missourians."[80]

At last, Porter was free. Despite the grand jury's ruling, Boggs insisted to his dying day that Porter was the one who fired the shot on that rainy February night.

But there was no welcoming committee as the emaciated Porter walked out of the jail. Doniphan warned of a plot against Porter's life, told him to stay off the main roads, and admonished him to travel only at night. Spending that first night at the nearby farmhouse of a sympathetic widow, Porter ate his first solid meal in more than nine months. The next morning Porter loaded his mother onto a coach to Nauvoo then spent the next eleven days fighting his way through deep snow and thick brush over a distance of almost three hundred miles. When he finally arrived at Crooked River, the skin was worn off his bleeding feet, and Porter paid a man fifty cents to carry him piggyback.

At Montrose, he crossed the river in a small boat. Finally arriving in Nauvoo on Christmas Day, 1843, Porter headed straight for the home of the man whose life he had defended: the Prophet Joseph Smith. By this time, Porter was quite a sight: even without the rigors of his eleven-day journey by foot, he had not had a change of clothes during the nine

Joseph Smith's Mansion House in Nauvoo, where Porter overheard the plot to martyr Joseph.

months he was in jail. Nor had his hair or beard been cut—not even washed. He was almost skeletally thin.

Peering through the windows of the Mansion House, Porter could see that a Christmas party was underway. Barging into the house, Porter looked so bad that Joseph didn't even recognize his old friend. Thinking the intruder was a drunk thug from Missouri, Joseph asked the police captain to take him outside. A scuffle ensued—even in his wretched condition, Porter was strong enough to stand his ground. Annoyed by the resistance, Joseph took off his coat and determined to remove the man himself. As he made eye contact with the supposed ruffian, Joseph later said, "To my great surprise and joy untold, I discovered it was my long-tried, warm, but cruelly persecuted friend, Orrin Porter Rockwell."[81]

Instead of throwing the man out, Joseph led him to the center of the parlor, sat him on a chair, and invited him to relate the story of his capture, imprisonment, acquittal, and return to Nauvoo. Sobered by Porter's story, the crowd fell silent. Emma brought him a large piece of pie. And Joseph Smith was moved to promise Porter that as long as he remained true to the Church and did not cut his hair or his beard, no bullet or blade would harm him.

From that day forward, Porter wore his long hair braided and tucked into a bob at the nape of his neck. He cut it only once: to have it made into a wig for Agnes Smith—the widow of Joseph Smith's younger brother, Don Carlos Smith—after she lost all her hair in a bout of typhoid fever.

Intent to resume his duties as Joseph's bodyguard, Porter remained with him through thick and thin—including destruction of the *Nauvoo Expositor*, a newspaper started by apostate Mormons who now decried Joseph as a fallen prophet. While Joseph himself issued the order, it was Porter who kicked in the door of the publishing company and helped destroy the press. It was one of the largest links in the chain of events that inevitably led to Carthage.

When authorities ordered Joseph, Hyrum, and Willard Richards to Carthage to answer charges that they destroyed the newspaper, the three complied. As they walked toward the river about 4 P.M., Joseph fell behind with Porter. When the others shouted to him to hurry, Joseph replied, "It is of no use to hurry, for we are going back to be slaughtered."[82] When Joseph asked to talk to the members of his church once more, Porter arranged for a meeting under the stars.

The next day, Porter mounted his horse and accompanied the three to the edge of town. As they prepared to leave Nauvoo, Joseph asked Porter to stay behind. As Joseph's personal bodyguard, Porter begged for the chance to accompany him but finally respected the Prophet's orders. Joseph had things for Porter to do.

Over the next several days, Porter stayed busy trying to plead the Prophet's case—or, that failing, help him escape. He shuttled petitions back and forth between Carthage and Nauvoo. He followed Joseph's instructions in trying to have one accuser arrested for perjury.[83] At one point he brought horses across the river under the cloak of darkness, ready to help Joseph start for the Rocky Mountains.[84]

Finally Joseph hastily penned an order from Carthage and had it carried and read to Porter: "Under no circumstances are you to come to Carthage. If you do, you will be killed."[85]

On the afternoon of June 27, 1844, Porter went to the Mansion House in Nauvoo to get his hat, which he had left in an upper room of the mansion. When he strolled into the room to fetch the hat, he saw Governor Thomas Ford and a large crowd of men gathered to hear someone standing behind a chair and speaking. Before the men in the room saw him and fell silent, he heard the speaker say, "The deed is done before this time."[86] Clearly he was referring to the murder of Joseph Smith.

Leaving the Mansion House, Porter ran into F. M. Higbee and accused him of seeking Joseph's life. Using some "very insulting language" in reply, Higbee denied the charge. At that point "a scuffle ensued, during which a letter dropped out of Higbee's hat, which stated that there were seventy of the mob ready in Iowa to come upon Nauvoo."[87]

Sadly, the deed *had* been done. When news of the Prophet's martyrdom reached Porter, he rushed to find Joseph's son. Weeping like a child, Porter cried, "They have killed the only friend I have ever had!"

As outlined in the history books, the remaining days in Nauvoo were punctuated with an air of desperation and a sense of chaos. Determined members of the Church finished construction of the Nauvoo Temple; Porter was endowed there on January 5, 1845, just six months after Joseph Smith was martyred. Since he was divorced and still single, he did not receive the sealing ordinance.

Tension in Nauvoo between Mormons and non-Mormons continued to escalate in the year following the Prophet's martyrdom. Late one afternoon, Porter and another man were delivering weapons to members of the Church when they stopped on the road for dinner. Passersby quickly ascertained that the two were Mormons and armed themselves with some weapons of their own: stones. They were poised and ready for the attack when the two men finished eating and climbed back into the wagon.

Porter told his companion to take the reins, then Porter stood in the wagon, his rifle resting on his shoulder. "Go ahead and throw your stones," he shouted, "and I'll throw lead."[88] The dumbfounded anti-Mormons dropped their stones and allowed Porter and his companion to ride peacefully out of town.

During the upheaval in Nauvoo, a rivalry between two sheriffs drew Porter into its ugly snare and resulted in his subsequent murder conviction. Hancock County sheriff Jacob Backenstos, who had been friendly and offered protection to the Mormons, was being chased by a mob intent on killing him. The mob, it appeared, was squarely on the other side of "the Mormon issue."

Fleeing from the mob in an effort to save himself, Backenstos suddenly saw his salvation: Porter Rockwell. Backenstos rapidly deputized Porter and asked for protection; still quite a distance from his target, Porter raised his gun and fired a single shot. Distance notwithstanding, the shot hit its target, killing the mob leader instantly.

Recognizing a skilled gunman when they saw one, the rest of the mob scattered. Porter must have felt a tinge of satisfaction: He had shot Peoria Sheriff Frank A. Worrell—leader of the Carthage Grays and the man tasked with protecting Joseph Smith the day he was killed.

Porter, suddenly finding himself a lawman, had now killed a lawman. It was a crime that would eventually work in favor of the Mormons in a most peculiar way.

When the earliest company of pioneers set out across the plains under the leadership of Church President Brigham Young, Porter Rockwell was with them—not only as a scout and pioneer himself, but as bodyguard to Brigham. He also served as Brigham's messenger, making his way back and forth across Iowa at least five times in the service of the prophet.

Then Brigham summoned Porter and asked the ultimate.

Apparently there were a number of Mormons left behind in Nauvoo who were still too impoverished to start on their journey. With most Mormons having left the city, the poorest ones were in a decided minority and were now the victims of blistering persecution. Brigham was desperate to find a way to distract the mobs and offer the beleaguered Saints a modicum of peace.

Porter offered that distraction. If he would go back to Nauvoo, urged Brigham, and get himself arrested for the murder of Frank Worrell, the mobs would focus their attention on Porter and forget about the penniless Mormons still living in the city. It was a horrific request—Porter's nine-month

Brigham Young

stint in the prison at Independence had almost killed him—but he determined to follow the prophet, who promised to hire a good lawyer to defend him.

It was a brilliant plot.

Word was sent ahead that Porter was returning to Nauvoo, so Mormons and non-Mormons alike knew he was coming (though the Mormons knew "the rest of the story," so to say). Galloping into town, Porter checked into a boardinghouse and then went outside, looking to cause some trouble that would attract attention.[89]

He didn't have to look far. Spotting an old enemy, Porter started chasing him through the streets, firing his pistols into the air above the man's head. To no one's surprise, lawmen took immediate notice and started chasing Porter, who was chasing his old enemy. Porter circled around, barged into the boardinghouse, and barricaded himself in his room.

It was a good, old-fashioned standoff. The Mormons in town were aware of Brigham's plan and only too happy to cooperate. Milling outside the boardinghouse with the rapidly gathering crowd, they approached the sheriff with "fears" that Porter—now a "loose cannon"—was in town and that he was sure to cause them trouble.

Their act played perfectly into the sheriff's hands. Thinking that even the Mormons were against Porter, the sheriff started gathering up a posse to storm the boardinghouse. Just before they were ready to break down the door, Porter surrendered and walked out with his hands raised high above his head.

The sheriff pounced and immediately stripped Porter of his weapons: two double-barreled sawed-off shotguns, one strapped to each side of Porter's body; a pair of Colt revolvers; a Bowie knife; and enough preloaded cylinders in his coat pockets that Porter could have fired seventy rounds without stopping to reload. It goes without saying that he was immediately thrown behind bars, charged with the murder of Frank Worrell—a capital offense that carried the death penalty.

Enter the promised lawyer. And what an irony *that* was. Porter was represented by Almon Babbitt, his first wife's divorce attorney. But not even that ruffled Porter; he was, after all, on a mission for the prophet.

During his stint in Independence, Porter had tried one thing after another to shorten his prison stay, including several escape attempts. This time he did everything he could to drag it out. Every day he remained behind bars was another day of respite for the Mormons still trying to clear out of Nauvoo. He managed to drag the time out to four months while he awaited trial.

Once the trial finally started, Babbitt's chief strategy was to call Backenstos to the stand and make a case for self-defense. It worked. Backenstos testified under oath that he had ordered Porter, by then deputized, to shoot Worrell to defend Backenstos himself from certain death. After a brief deliberation, the jury declared Porter innocent on the grounds of self-defense.

Backenstos was later tried for the murder of Worrell in a separate trial. Like Porter, he was acquitted—partly because the killing was "altogether justifiable," and partly because no one knew for certain which man had actually fired the fatal shot. That was the company line. In actuality, no one tried to keep the matter secret. It was "common knowledge" in Nauvoo and later in Utah that Porter Rockwell had pulled the trigger and "saved the officer's life."[90] Perhaps it had also been a small taste of sweet revenge on Porter's part against the man who had failed to protect Joseph.

Acquitted of charges in Worrell's murder, Porter headed back to Winter Quarters, where he joined Brigham Young's vanguard company of about a hundred men and fewer women. Their purpose was to leave the boundaries of the United States and find a new home for the Mormons . . . and Brigham asked Porter to be the lead scout and

The ox yoke used by Porter Rockwell when he traveled with Brigham's vanguard company.

hunter. In that capacity, Porter scouted out the Mormon Trail, which would later lead thousands to their new home in the Rockies. His eyesight was so keen that he could often see landmarks two or three days before others in the company could see the same things.

Porter eventually led the vanguard company to the summit of East Canyon, overlooking the Salt Lake Valley—the precise spot Brigham Young had wanted to explore. To the rest of the world, it was a Godforsaken slice of land. To Brigham Young and his followers, it was a spot God had preserved for them—a safe harbor and refuge from the enemies who had so relentlessly pursued them.

Porter's scouting days were far from over as the vanguard company settled in and started the blistering work of turning the desert into a rose. Porter traveled back to Nebraska with Brigham Young, then spent almost a year at Brigham's request traveling throughout the territory on a peacekeeping mission to the Indians in the area. Porter engineered a pack train full of trade goods, gifts that enabled him to make friends with and earn the respect of the Indians.

When Porter returned from that assignment, he renewed his acquaintance with John Neff, whose family he had met in one of the wagon trains. John's daughter, Mary Ann, caught Porter's eye; better yet, she returned his affection. They were sealed in Brigham Young's parlor, since the Endowment House had not yet been constructed, and Brigham himself hosted the wedding party. (Porter subsequently married two more times after being widowed twice.) It was a hasty celebration: the very next day, Brigham sent Porter fifty miles south to Nephi on yet another assignment to the Indians, this one to execute a peace treaty with the Utes.

By this time, Porter's reputation as a bodyguard was legendary, and he was appointed to guard the territorial sheriff. Immediately after the sheriff's election in 1849, he deputized Porter as deputy marshal for the Territory of Deseret—a region larger than the present-day state of Utah—making him one of Utah's earliest lawmen. It was a position he held until his death. Only the most brazen and foolhardy criminals challenged Porter: he was relentless in getting his man, and his endurance was almost mythical. While other lawmen sauntered along a trail, walking their horses as they searched for clues, Porter followed each trail in his buckboard at an aggressive gallop, never giving up.[91]

And that's where the distinction started to blur . . . or did it? In his tireless efforts as a lawman, he sometimes seemed to be more of an outlaw . . . or did he? While the collective body count of the authentic Mormon outlaws could well-nigh be counted on the fingers of one hand, Porter was never shy about taking aim and firing. As mentioned, he is the only gunman to have killed more outlaws than Tom Horn, Bat Masterson, Doc Holladay, and Wyatt Earp combined. It was known far and wide that no one could kill Porter, and men occasionally came from as far away as California just to try. No one succeeded, fulfilling the prophecy uttered by Joseph Smith.

The stories are so thick they practically beg to be told. And none of them lack color. Take, for example, the story involving Loren Dibble, a kid with too much confidence and not enough good sense. An outlaw who was known as a pretty good marksman, Dibble decided— apparently on nothing more than principle—that he was just the man to take down Porter Rockwell.

One day he got his chance. In broad daylight right on Main Street in downtown Lehi, Dibble started firing at Porter. Despite his reputed acumen, every bullet missed its mark—even from a short distance. Porter waited until Dibble had emptied his guns before reaching for his own firearms. The explosion of gunfire split the air as Porter fired again and again at Dibble's feet, causing him leap back and forth in a frenetic and desperate dance. Porter finally replaced his guns in their holsters, walked over to Dibble, and shoved him forcefully to the ground.

Then, shaking the kid like a rag doll, Porter spewed in disgust, "If I didn't know your father, you'd be a dead man right now."

Brigham Young's nephew, Lot Huntington—himself a small-time outlaw—wasn't so lucky. It seems that prominent Taylorsville resident John Bennion had ridden his horse, one of the finest in the territory, to tithing settlement at his bishop's house. He came out to find that his horse was missing. Just like that. Stolen. Right in front of the bishop's house. And during tithing settlement, no less.

John knew just what to do: He sent for Porter Rockwell.

Porter knew just what to do too. He started the pursuit along with Bennion, Bennion's son Sam, and two others. An expert tracker, Porter followed the trail to Camp Floyd, some distance to the south, and started asking around. Sure enough, Lot Huntington and a couple of other two-bit outlaws had been there earlier with John Bennion's horse. They were nowhere to be found, so Porter kept following the trail to where it ended: Faust Station, a Pony Express station in present-day Tooele County. It was after 4 A.M. when they arrived; Porter stationed the others around the bunkhouse while he hid himself behind the woodpile.

At sunup, as the men inside finished breakfast, station manager Henry J. Faust—a convert to the Mormon Church from Germany and part-time Pony Express rider—emerged from the bunkhouse to throw out the dishwater. Porter quietly caught Faust's attention and ordered him to tell the outlaws at the breakfast table that they were under arrest for stealing the horse. As soon as they heard who was outside, two of the outlaws immediately emerged, hands in the air.

Not so with Lot Huntington. He was tough, and he thought he could easily outsmart Porter. He couldn't have been more wrong. He finally came out of the bunkhouse and held his gun on Porter while he walked to the corral, threatening to kill Porter unless he was allowed to get away. Porter answered quietly, "Lot, don't make me kill you." But Huntington was undeterred.

He led Bennion's horse out of the corral, positioning the horse between him and Porter, still keeping Porter in the crosshairs of his pistol. But then things went south. The horse bumped its nose on the corral railing, which startled it. It reared, leaving Lot exposed. Porter took aim and shot Lot directly through the heart. Lot Huntington fell backward against the corral fence. He didn't have a chance. Even if Porter *did* know his uncle.

Incidentally, Porter turned down Bennion's offer of a reward, to be paid in gold, protesting that he captured and returned Bennion's horse while in the line of duty.

Then there were the horse thieves who decided they could get away with all of Porter's horses in one smooth operation. Arriving at one of Porter's ranches late one night, knowing Porter was nowhere in the vicinity, the three galloped up to the ranch house and loudly demanded to be let in. As soon as the caretaker timidly opened the door and told the outlaws they could come in, they started shooting. He dived back inside and blew out the lantern while the thieves got away with all the horses.

When Porter arrived the next day to news of the theft, Porter growled, "Always shoot first, then offer to let them in. That way, they know you're armed."

No matter that almost a full day had gone by. Porter was back in the saddle, pounding off into the distance to find his horses—and the thieves who had stolen them. Hours later he was back—alone—with not only his own horses but those of the horse thieves as well. The thieves, he explained vaguely, wouldn't be back—they were "face-down in a wash" somewhere.

Porter was often hired by Wells Fargo to ride shotgun alongside the stages carrying gold shipments. On one such occasion, he was waiting at Faust Station to meet the coach when he saw it come barreling over the horizon from Lookout Pass, going far faster than it should. When the stage screeched to a halt at Faust Station, the breathless driver broke the bad news: he'd been robbed.

Apparently he was on his scheduled route through the west desert when he rounded the road near Riverbed and came upon a dead man facedown in the middle of the road. Leaving the coach to investigate, he used the toe of his boot to turn the man over. But the man *wasn't* dead: He leaped to his feet, thrust a gun in the face of the driver, and took the strongbox with its gold—an amount approaching two million dollars in today's value.

Porter set off on his own to apprehend the thief. Arriving at Riverbed, where the stage had been robbed, he picked up the outlaw's tracks, heading south and east to Cherry Creek. Staying hidden in the

The ruins of Porter Rockwell's house near Crystal Hot Lakes.

hills above the creek, Porter saw a man making camp at the river's edge. Staying awake around the clock for several days, Porter never let the man out of his sight. His vigil was rewarded: After breakfast one morning, the man took a shovel into the cedar trees and started digging. As he was about to bury the last bar of gold bullion, Porter shoved a revolver in his back, arrested him, and transported the thief and the gold to his ranch.

By the time Porter arrived at his ranch it was late evening, and he was exhausted—he'd been awake around the clock for days while he watched to see what the outlaw was going to do with the gold. Leaving the outlaw in custody of his foreman, Porter retired for some much-needed sleep. Unfortunately, so did the foreman. The outlaw made a hasty escape and mounted a horse that was tied up outside.

The commotion woke Porter, who launched out the door and fired a shot into the black darkness. The shot was immediately followed by a scream. But neither Porter nor the foreman, armed with lanterns, could find hide nor hair of the outlaw. He got clean away.

Porter delivered the gold to Wells Fargo in Salt Lake a week later and apologized for letting the outlaw slip through his fingers. But as it turns out, that's not exactly what happened. A short time later, riders discovered a dead man along a telegraph route, a large bullet hole in his side. Porter had brought down his man after all—from a distance, and in pitch dark.

Porter didn't *always* shoot first and ask questions later. Take the case of Frank Karrick, a businessman who hauled freight between Sacramento and Salt Lake City. He was camped about seventy miles south of Salt Lake when he discovered nine mules and a valuable stallion missing. He tried to find the animals on his own but lost the trail after about forty miles. It was clearly a job for Porter Rockwell.

Karrick took Porter to the very spot where he had lost the trail. Porter slid out of the saddle, focused with intensity on the area for a few minutes, and suddenly jumped back into the saddle. He rode so furiously that Karrick had a difficult time keeping up.

By sunset the next day, Porter and Karrick arrived at the campsite of the two rustlers; Karrick's mules were still tied up nearby. Porter crept quietly up to the campfire, whipped out his Colt revolver, and ordered the surprised outlaws to thrust their hands in the air.

Lucky for them, they did as they were asked.

Porter turned down Karrick's offer of cash—a *lot* of cash—for rescuing the livestock. But Karrick wasn't one to let a gallant deed go unrewarded. Porter later received a shipment from California consisting of a finely tooled leather saddle and a gallon of California's finest whisky.

It's tough for some to label Porter an outlaw, since all of his shootings were apparently done in the line of duty—but there was the mysterious and somewhat troublesome case of the Aiken brothers. With that one, the waters got muddied.

John and William Aiken were two of a group of six veteran gamblers who started out in California and made their way to Utah en route to find Johnston's army in Wyoming. They had a few things on their agenda. They wanted to establish a gambling house, saloon, and house of prostitution right in the heart of Zion, businesses they figured would appeal to the soldiers who would soon be arriving in the Territory. But that's not all: first and foremost, the talented gamblers intended on swindling the soldiers out of their earnings.

When they arrived in Salt Lake, Brigham Young decided to put a stop to it all. He didn't want those kinds of business establishments getting a toehold in his territory. Besides that, he figured the group already knew too much about what the Mormons were planning against the army—and they were the type who would be only too eager to sell the information at the right price. Two of the six left the territory on their own, with promises not to intercept the army. The other four were escorted to Lehi and turned over to Porter Rockwell, Sylvanus Collett, and two other men, who promised to take them south to Nevada and back to California.

Sylvanus Collett, who went with Porter to escort the Aiken brothers.

That's where things get a little murky. The group traveled through Nephi and camped on the Sevier River. Two were apparently killed out on the desert. The other two showed up in Nephi a few days later, bloodied and battered. They too were killed a few days later as they tried to get back to Salt Lake.

No one knew exactly what happened. At first the deaths were blamed on the Indians—not exactly an unknown occurrence during those times. Anti-Mormon newspapers then stirred up a rumor blaming the deaths on Brigham Young and the Mormons. The motive? Greed. The gamblers, it was reported, were carrying a large stash of gold coins.

The story eventually died down, and no one was arrested—not then, at least. Porter never discussed what happened to the Aiken brothers. Neither did any of the other three escorts.

Fast-forward twenty years. John D. Lee had just been executed for his role in the Mountain Meadows Massacre, and officials figured they could nab Porter on the Aiken murders. In 1877, he was indicted on two charges of first-degree murder, was arrested, and spent six days in jail before being allowed to post bail. He had only one response to what had happened twenty years earlier to the Aikens: "All is fine." He died before the case came to trial in October 1878, a proceeding in which Sylvanus Collett was acquitted.

Though he could never read or write, Porter was a successful and prolific businessman. He owned the Hot Springs Brewery Hotel at the point of the mountain, sold whiskey he manufactured himself to mining camps as far north as Montana, bred a special strain of horses sold as far away as Peru, and raised horses and cattle at a bustling ranch

The ruins of buildings at Porter's Government Creek ranch.

called Government Creek. He eventually owned the entire tract of land from Skull Valley to the site of the current-day Little Sahara Sand Dunes near Eureka, a vast swath of incalculable value. At his death, his estate was estimated at close to two million dollars in today's currency.

Orrin Porter Rockwell died at the age of sixty-five of a heart attack while awaiting trial on the Aiken murder charges. After attending a play the evening of Saturday, June 8, 1878, he spent a few hours drinking at a favorite saloon. He spent most of the day Sunday in bed, feeling very ill. At 5 P.M. he suddenly got up, pulled on his boots, then fell back into bed, dead. Suspecting that he had been poisoned at the saloon, an autopsy was performed and confirmed the cause of death as a heart attack.

An editorial in the *Salt Lake Tribune*, very anti-Mormon at the time, said of Porter:

> He killed unsuspecting travelers, whose booty was coveted by his prophet-master. He killed fellow Saints who held secrets that menaced the safety of their fellow criminals in the priesthood. He killed Apostates who dared to wag their tongues about the wrongs they had endured. And he killed mere sojourners in Zion merely to keep his hand in.[92]

The *Tribune* reported that he had participated in at least a hundred murders. His funeral, held at his ward meetinghouse, was attended by more than a thousand people. Apostle and future Church President Joseph F. Smith spoke, going as far afield as possible from the *Tribune* editorial and saying the following about Porter:

> They say he was a murderer; if he was he was the friend of Joseph Smith and Brigham Young, and he was faithful to them, and to his covenants, and he has gone to Heaven. . . . Porter Rockwell was yesterday afternoon ushered into Heaven clothed with

Orrin Porter Rockwell shortly before his death in 1878.

immortality and eternal life, and crowned with all glory which belongs to a departed saint. He has his little faults but Porter's life on earth, taken altogether, was one worthy of example, and reflected honor upon the church. Through all his trials he never once forgot his obligations to his brethren and his God.

He is buried in the Salt Lake City Cemetery.

Orrin Porter Rockwell's headstone in the Salt Lake City Cemetery.

EPILOGUE
The Lawmen

WELL, NOW YOU SHOULD KNOW a little more about the Mormon out-laws than you did when you first picked up this book. But they're only part of the story. If you think the Mormon outlaws were an interesting bunch, you should have seen the Mormon lawmen who pursued them.

The tightly knit sheriffs, constables, deputies, marshals, and police chiefs who patrolled the Old West in search of outlaws of the day were a well-pedigreed bunch. Most were Mormons, through and through, and had the history to prove it. Their families came from Scandinavia and Europe, some of the earliest converts to Mormonism. They put

down roots in Nauvoo. And they were a homogenous bunch. You didn't have to go far up any branches of the family tree to see that most were solidly connected to the same sturdy trunk.

Take Californian John A. Bascom, for example. His ancestors consist of an astonishing number of lawmen, all on the same family tree, who chased the likes of Butch Cassidy and Matt Warner. His grandfather John W. Bascom was the deputy sheriff of Uintah County; other relatives in that line included lawmen Wal Lybbert, Dave Manwaring, Kimbell Bascom, and Ally Bascom. His great-grandfather on

Uintah County Sheriff John W. Bascom, 1895

one side, Joel Almon Bascom, was chief of police in Provo and later town marshal in Mona. His great-grandfather on the other side, C. F. B. Lybbert, was town marshal in Levan during the time Matt Warner saddled up to join Butch Cassidy's gang. He later served as a judge in Naples, just outside Vernal.

Relationships among the lawmen themselves were literal.

And when it came to the relationship between the law and the outlaws, this group elevated it to a whole new level.

The outlaws may have been on "the other side" of the commandments—secular and spiritual—when it came to the lawmen, but the two groups were often thicker than thieves, so to say. William Bascom, later to go down in history as a ferocious lawman, was one of Butch Cassidy's best friends. Shucks, he even rode now and then with the Wild Bunch. Only for the adventure, of course—not to break the law.

Oh, by the way, that was the same William Bascom who gave fugitives David Lant and Harry Tracy his horse so they could evade four rapidly approaching deputies intent on cuffing Lant and Tracy. That's not all: Bascom in essence chose up sides for a holler-off. The four who

were in pursuit were all members of his own family—William Preece, John Bascom, Wal Lybbert, and David Manwaring.

Some of the Lybbert boys, later to become well-respected lawmen, slept many nights in the granary on the Lybbert Ranch right alongside the outlaws. And why not? Sure, the Lybberts knew the "others" were sort of "rowdy," but had no real idea what they were doing. After all, no newspapers were tossed on the front

Waldemar "Wal" Lybbert, who taught David Lant to shear sheep.

Photo of the family of lawman and judge C. F. B. Lybbert taken in 1897 in front of the Lybbert ranch log cabin. The granary, where members of the Wild Bunch slept, is behind this house. C. F. B. Lybbert is seated in the middle between his two wives. Standing on the far left is Enoch Lybbert, a deputized posse member. Standing on the far right is Uintah County deputy sheriff Waldemar "Wal" Lybbert. Standing in the middle with the mustache is Uintah County deputy sheriff John W. Bascom. (All photos in this chapter courtesy of John A. Bascom, Apple Valley, CA.)

porch every morning. No one had access to the nightly news. That's not all: the outlaws were fun, friendly, polite—and they had lots of money, which they didn't mind spending on whoever needed a pick-me-up.

Even when the law-abiding guys figured out what the others were up to, they stuck around. After all, the outlaws were considered to be nothing more

than "wayward Mormon boys"—their day's equivalent of the slightly rebellious youth who manages to get a pack of smokes from an older kid down the street. No worries. They'll eventually come to their senses, the Lybberts (and everyone else) figured. No big deal.

And most of the outlaws came from good families—the ones you went to church with, the kind of people you *want* living next door. And so it was that the Bascoms, eventually some of the best-known and most well-respected lawmen in the territory, didn't give a second thought to the Swazy boys next door. Their father not only owned the biggest hotel in Mona but one of Provo's biggest banks. He was an upstanding member of society in every way imaginable. Never mind that his three boys—tipping the scales at a combined thousand pounds—created all sorts of havoc in a decidedly outlaw flair. They practically made cattle rustling an art form. But who cared? They were *friends*. Next-door neighbors.

(And, just so you know, the Swazy boys weren't the only ones with a flair for breaking the law. When the polygamist hotel-bank owner died, his youngest wife took off with the bank president—and all the money.)

There was often a "what's mine is yours" attitude between the law and the outlaws. Joel Almon Bascom Jr. owned and operated the Bascom Hotel in Naples. He freely rented rooms to Butch Cassidy and a slew of other outlaws, even though he was a deputy and son of the chief of police. It was just proper courtesy, after all.

The proper, law-abiding Mormon women went right along with the lawmen in their attitudes toward the outlaws. Keep in mind, John Bascom reminds us, that many of the outlaws' exploits and activities were

Joel Almon Bascom

never known by the Church women. They simply knew the outlaws as "wayward boys," the sons of people with whom they attended church. They were neighbors. Their children went to school with these boys. They were all, so to say, one big, happy family.

Some of the lawmen didn't completely turn the other cheek, even

though they didn't exactly slap on the handcuffs, either. Deputy Waldemar ("Wal") Lybbert spent his time breaking horses and shearing sheep at Brown's Hole. Obviously, his friends and neighbors in the Hole included a fair share of guys who were skirting around the law, to put it mildly. But he knew outlaws long before he drifted into the Hole—he

Bronc Bustin' Bascom Boys, from left, John, Ramond, Earl, Mel, and Weldon, 1939.

Earl W. Bascom

had lived around the corner from Matt Warner and just two blocks down the street from Tom McCarty. The three were lifelong friends.

With so many good friends who were . . . um . . . on the other side of the fence when it came to the law, Wal Lybbert had a soft spot in his heart for the boys who had gone a little bad. As a result, he often tried to spare the rod and spoil the outlaw. He could tell David Lant was moving rapidly toward trouble—and not just a little trouble. So Wal took the young man under his wing and taught him the fine art of sheep shearing. Wal saw it as a way to help Lant go straight with a legitimate way to earn a living. Lant saw it as a lot of hot, smelly, sweaty, undignified labor. You have to give Lybbert snaps for trying, even though Lant decided it was lots easier to steal than to shear.

The world of the outlaws often intersected that of the law in very peculiar ways. When lawman Porter Merrill bought a ranch on the Green River, the adobe walls of the ranch house were riddled with bullet holes. Why? The outlaws who owned the ranch before him used their idle hours to shoot at flies. Lawmen and brothers Milby and Isaac Lybbert were fascinated with a cabin they found on Blue Mountain near Cassidy Point. Burned into the inside walls were all the popular cattle brands of the day—along with do-it-yourself illustrations on how rustlers could "change" the brands. No sweat. Building your own herd was just a branding iron away.

There were even little spots here and there where no lawmen had jurisdiction. They simply stood back, rubbed their whiskered chins, and shook their heads. Take as an example the piece of land known only as "The Strip." About a hundred yards wide and half a mile long, it had been taken away from the Indian reservation by the federal government. But thanks to an oversight—you know how these things can happen—the government failed to cede it back to the state or any other government entity. No lawmen could arrest anyone on that little strip of land, which was crowded with saloons and all other kinds of unsavory establishments. Might as well all be friends.

Because of the dogged efforts of the Mormon lawmen, we have been able to follow the trail of many lesser-known Mormon outlaws. They were trails that definitely led away from Utah: As Brigham Young called Mormons to colonize the western part of the United States and Canada, the outlaws naturally followed.

Their names aren't easily recognized, and they weren't given real estate in this book, but they had interesting tales to tell. There was Charlie Martin, part of a gang out of Joshua Tree, California, and one of dozens of Mormon outlaws who went to prison for stealing horses. Quite a few of those Mormon horse thieves found the hangman's noose around their necks.

Then there were Charles Atwood and Mark Collett. They were part of the twenty or so Mormons who rode with Butch Cassidy. But when a band of Mormons headed north under Brigham's direction, this pair of outlaws broke away from the Wild Bunch and tore up part of Canada before landing in jail up north.

And there was Joe Gurr, who was finally released from prison only to find that his wife had taken up with another man—the proud owner of a new Browning nine-shot semiautomatic. What Joe expected to be a homecoming celebration degenerated into something much less merry. Let's just say that during the ensuing struggle, in which Joe was armed with a mere six-shooter, he died with nine bullets in his body.

There you have it. When it comes to the stuff of fancy, few chapters in history can compare with the Wild West. And when it comes to the stuff of legend, few can compete with the Mormon outlaws—and lawmen—who so thoroughly owned that landscape.

It's an era we'll not see again . . . an illusion we can only imagine. But what fun that illusion is—and how worth remembering! As the sage Mark Twain reminded us, "Don't part with your illusions. When they are gone you may still exist, but you have ceased to live."

ENDNOTES

1. Terry Abraham, "Utah Saints and Sinners: Mormons and Outlaws," *Western Historical Quarterly*, 1979. Many thanks to Abraham for his keen observations, which informed much of this chapter.

2. Wallace Stegner, *Mormon Country* (New York: Duell, Sloan & Pearce, 1942), 285.

3. U.S. Bureau of the Census. *Historical Statistics of the United States, Colonial Times to 1957* (Washington, D.C., 1960).

4. See Leonard J. Arrington, *Great Basin Kingdom: An Economic History of the Latter-Day Saints, 1830–1900* (Cambridge, MA: Harvard University Press, 1958).

5. J. W. Gunnison, *The Mormons, or Latter-Day Saints, in the Valley of the Great Salt Lake* (Philadelphia, PA: Lippincott, 1856), 66.

6. George W. France, *The Struggles for Life and Home in the North-West by a Pioneer Homebuilder; Life, 1865–1889* (New York: I. Goldmann, 1890), 60–61.

7. J. H. Beadle, *Western Wilds* (Cincinnati, OH: Jones Brothers, 1879), 102.

8. Gunnison, 160.

9. Quoted by Juanita Brooks, *John Doyle Lee* (Glendale, CA: Arthur H. Clark, 1962), 92.

10. Quoted in *Utah: A Guide to the State* (New York: Hastings House, 1941), 388.

11. *Utah: A Guide to the State*, 326.

12. Charles Kelly, *The Outlaw Trail* (New York: Bonanza Books, 1959), 11.

13. Kelly, 33.

14. Kelly, 11.

15. See T. W. Adorno, et al., *The Authoritarian Personality* (New York: Harper, 1950).

16. William Mulder, *Homeward to Zion* (Minneapolis, MN: University of Minnesota Press, 1957), 221.

17. See Adorno, 759.

18. See Adorno, 889.

19. John Wesley Powell, *Canyons of the Colorado* (Meadville, PA: Flood and Vincent, 1895).

20. LeRoy R. Hafen and Ann W. Hafen, eds., *To the Rockies and Oregon 1839–1842, The Far West and Rockies Historical Series*, Vol. III (Glendale, CA: The Arthur H. Clark Co., 1955), 136–137.

21. Dick Dunham and Vivian Dunham, *Flaming Gorge Country* (Denver, CO: Eastwood Printing and Publishing Company, 1977), 49.

22. Jesse S. Hoy, "The J. S. Hoy Manuscript," Colorado State University Library, Ft. Collins, Colorado, 90.

23. Frank Waters, *The Colorado* (New York: Holt, Rinehart, and Winston, 1946), 177.

24. Obadiah Oakley, *Expedition to Oregon* (Fairfield, WA: Nabu Press, 1967), 17.

25. Thomas J. Farnham, *Travels in the Great Western Prairies, the Anahuac and Rocky Mountains, and in the Oregon Territory* (Poughkeepsie, NY, 1841), 59.

26. Frederick A. Wislizenus, *A Journey to the Rocky Mountains in the Year 1839* (St. Louis, MO: Missouri Historical Society, 1912), 129.

27. William T. Hamilton, *My Sixty Years on the Plains: Trapping, Trading, and Indian Fighting* (Norman, OK: Kessinger Publishing, 1960), 84–85.

28. Ann Bassett Willis, "'Queen Ann' of Brown's Park," *Colorado Magazine*, Vol. 26 (April 1952), 84.

29. Ann Zwinger, *Run, River, Run: A Naturalist's Journey Down One of the Great Rivers of the West* (Tucson, AZ: University of Arizona Press, 1975), 141.

30. Michael Rutter, *Outlaw Tales of Utah: True Stories of Utah's Most Famous Robbers, Rustlers, and Bandits* (Guilford, CT; The Globe Pequot Press, 2003), 38–39.

31. Lula Parker Betenson, *Butch Cassidy, My Brother* (Provo, UT: Brigham Young University Press, 1975), 80.

32. See Michael Rutter, *Outlaw Tales of Utah: True Stories of Utah's Most Famous Robbers, Rustlers, and Bandits* (Guilford, CT; The Globe Pequot Press, 2003), 46–47.

33. Some of the information on Robbers' Roost was adapted from Charles Kelly, *The Outlaw Trail: A History of Butch Cassidy and His Wild Bunch* (Salt Lake City, 1938); Jeffrey D. Nichols, "Robbers' Roost Outlaw Trail," *History Blazer*, August 1995; and Richard Patterson, *Historical Atlas of the Outlaw West*, 2nd ed. (Boulder, CO: Johnson Books, 1985).

34. See Rutter, 87.

35. Information on Butch Cassidy's pioneer heritage adapted from W. J. "Bill" Betenson, *Butch Cassidy, My Uncle: A Family Portrait* (Glendo, WY: High Plains Press, 2012), 17–28.

36. See Lula Parker Betenson, *Butch Cassidy, My Brother* (Provo, UT: Brigham Young University Press, 1975), 34.

37. Betenson, *Butch Cassidy, My Brother*, 24.

38. Charles A. Siringo, *A Cowboy Detective*, 1st ed. (Chicago, IL: W. B. Conkey Company, 1912), 351.

39. Richard Patterson, *Butch Cassidy: A Biography* (New York: John Wiley and Sons, 2007).

40. Matt Warner et al., *The Last of the Bandit Riders . . . Revisited* (Salt Lake City: Big Moon Traders, 2000).

41. Ann Bassett, 228–230.

42. *Dolores Star*, Dolores, Colorado, February 11, 1938.

43. Betenson, *Butch Cassidy, My Uncle*, 44.

44. Warner et al., *The Last of the Bandit Riders*, 121–122; and Betenson, *Butch Cassidy, My Uncle*, 44.

45. Tom McCarty, *Tom McCarty's Own Story* (Hamilton, MT: Rocky Mountain House Press, 1985), 28.

46. *Dolores Star*, February 11, 1938.

47. Monte Morland Rambler, "The Telluride Bank Holdup," *Shenandoah Tribune*, no date, as cited in Betenson, *Butch Cassidy, My Uncle*, 46.

48. Betenson, *Butch Cassidy, My Brother*, 179.

49. Larry Pointer, *In Search of Butch Cassidy* (Norman, OK: University of Oklahoma Press, 1977).

50. Information for the fight scene adapted from Rutter, 121–122.

51. Warner et al., 7.

52. Warner et al., 18.

53. Theodore Roosevelt, *Hunting the Grisly and Other Sketches,* Chapter 9, "In Cowboy Land" (originally published in 1900).

54. Warner et al., 15.

55. Warner et al., 86.

56. Warner et al., 87.

57. Warner et al., 20.

58. Warner et al., 124.

59. Warner et al., 125.

60. Warner et al., 6.

61. *Salt Lake Tribune,* May 4, 2003.

62. The description of the probable getaway route adapted from Richard Patterson, *Butch Cassidy: A Biography,* 1st ed. (Norman, OK: University of Oklahoma Press, 1998), 39–40.

63. Patterson, 39–40.

64. Much of this chapter relies on the careful research of Ellison as contained in Douglas W. Ellison, *David Lant: The Vanished Outlaw,* 1st ed. (Aberdeen, SD: Douglas W. Ellison, 1988).

65. Ellison, 30–31.

66. Charles Kelly, *The Outlaw Trail: A History of Butch Cassidy and His Wild Bunch* (Lincoln, NE: University of Nebraska Press, 1938), 189.

67. Ellison, 46.

68. Ellison, 58.

69. *History of the Church* 5:125.

70. John W. Rockwell and Jerry Borrowman, *Stories from the Life of Porter Rockwell* (American Fork, UT: Covenant Communications, Inc., 2010), xix.

71. B. H. Roberts, *Comprehensive History of the Church,* 4:279–280.

72. Richard L. Bushman, *Joseph Smith: Rough Stone Rolling* (New York: Knopf, 2005), 342–343.

73. Harold Schindler, *Orrin Porter Rockwell: Man of God, Son of Thunder,* 1st ed. (Salt Lake City, UT: University of Utah Press, 1993), 39.

74. *History of the Church* 3:251–254.

75. *History of the Church* 3:292.

76. *History of the Church* 3:320–322.

77. *History of the Church* 4:80–81.

78. Rockwell and Borrowman, 43.

79. Lawrence Cummins, "Orrin Porter Rockwell," *Friend*, May 1984, 42.

80. *Documentary History of the Church* 5:305; Joseph Fielding Smith, *Teachings of the Prophet Joseph Smith* (Salt Lake City: Deseret Book, 1977), 285.

81. *History of the Church* 6:134–135.

82. *History of the Church* 6:551.

83. Joseph Fielding Smith, *Church History and Modern Revelation* (Salt Lake City: Deseret Book, 1946), 4:186.

84. Joseph Fielding Smith Jr., *Doctrines of Salvation* (Salt Lake City: Bookcraft), 3:335.

85. *History of the Church* 6:565.

86. *History of the Church* 6:588.

87. *History of the Church* 7:130.

88. Adapted from Rockwell and Borrowman, 83.

89. This incident adapted from Rockwell and Borrowman, 87–89.

90. *History of the Church* 2:482

91. Cummins, 42.

92. Schindler, 367–368.

ABOUT THE AUTHOR

THE MANAGING EDITOR AT COVENANT COMMUNICATIONS, Kathryn Jenkins Gordon has had thirty-nine years of professional experience in corporate and internal communications, public relations, media relations, marketing communications, and publications management. She has been a press secretary for a US Congressman; vice-president of a Salt Lake City publishing company; manager of strategic communications for Novell, Inc.; director of public relations at a private college in Salt Lake City; and has held communications management positions at a variety of national and international corporations.

Former president-elect of the Association of Utah Publishers, she was also on the board of directors of the Mental Health Association of Utah County and the Constitutional Principles Policy Council. She has held membership in a number of local and national organizations and is the author or coauthor of more than eight dozen published books. A former member of Sigma Delta Chi, she was named an Outstanding Young Woman of America.

Her interests include reading, writing, cooking, traveling, and doing family history. She has met five presidents of the United States, sailed up the Nile River, prayed in the Garden of Gethsemane, eaten tempura in Tokyo, and received a dozen long-stemmed red roses from a stranger on the street in Athens.

She and her husband, Glenn, parent a combined family of ten children and five grandchildren.